Vacation, Retirement & Leisure HOME PLANS

GARLINGHOUSE

Submit all Canadian plan orders to:
The Garlinghouse Company
20 Cedar Street North
Kitchener, Ontario N2H 2WB

Canadians Order only: 1-800-561-4169
Fax#: 1-519-743-1282
Customer Service#: 1-519-743-4169

Library of Congress No.: 92-075089

ISBN: 0-938708-46-5

TABLE OF CONTENTS

Photography by Jeff Grant

Ranch Incorporates Victorian Features

No. 20058

This wonderful Victorian-featured Ranch design incorporates many luxury conveniences usually offered in larger designs. The master bedroom is expansive, with an oversized full bath complete with a walk-in closet, an individual shower, a full tub, and a two-sink wash basin. A large kitchen area is offered with a built-in island for convenience. The kitchen also has its own breakfast area. Located next to the kitchen is a half-bath. The living area is separated from the dining room by a half-wall partition. Two large bedrooms complete the interior of the house. They have large closets and share a full bath. A two-car garage and a wood deck complete the options listed in this design.

Main living area — 1,787 sq. ft.
Basement — 1,787 sq. ft.
Garage — 484 sq. ft.

Total living area — 1,787 sq. ft.

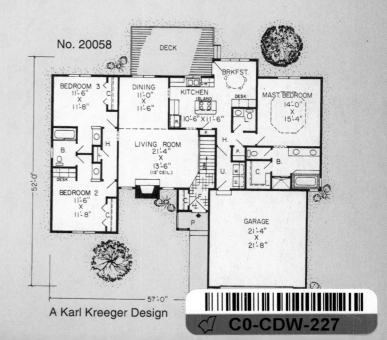

A Karl Kreeger Design

C0-CDW-227

Open Plan Accented by Loft, Windows & Deck

No. 10515

The first-floor living space of this inviting home blends the family room and dining room for comfortable family living. The large kitchen shares a preparation/eating bar with the dining room. The ample utility room is designed with a pantry, plus room for a freezer, washer and dryer. Also on the first floor is the master suite with its two closets and five piece bath which opens into a greenhouse. The second floor is highlighted by a loft which overlooks the first floor living area. The two upstairs bedrooms each have double closets and share a four-piece, compartmentalized bath.

First floor — 1,280 sq. ft.
Second floor — 735 sq. ft.
Greenhouse — 80 sq. ft.
Playhouse — 80 sq. ft.

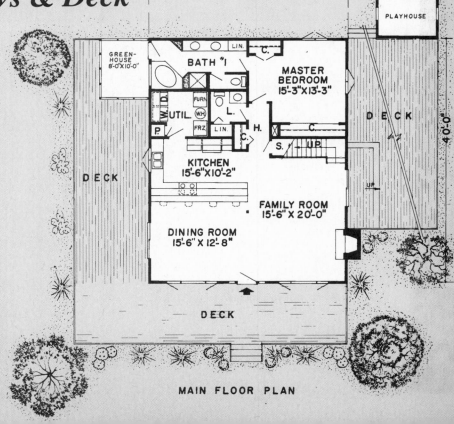

MAIN FLOOR PLAN

Total living area — 2,015 sq. ft.

Photography by John Ehrenclou

SECOND FLOOR PLAN

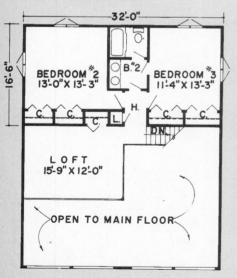

32'-0"

16'-6"

BEDROOM #2
13'-0" X 13'-3"

B. #2

BEDROOM #3
11'-4" X 13'-3"

C   C   C   H.   C   C
L.
DN.

LOFT
15'-9" X 12'-0"

OPEN TO MAIN FLOOR

No. 10515

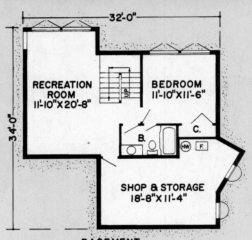

BASEMENT

*T*hree Levels of Spacious Living

First floor — 886 sq. ft.
Second floor — 456 sq. ft.
Basement — 886 sq. ft.

Total living area — 1,342 sq. ft.

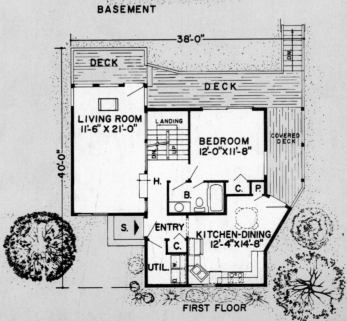

FIRST FLOOR

No. 10396

This passive solar design is suitable for vacation or year round living. The rear or southern elevation of the home is highlighted by an abundance of decks and glass. A minimum of windows are found on the north, east and west sides. The basement level has a large shop, storage and recreation areas, plus a bedroom. The first level living room is two steps up from the rest of the first floor, with two stories of glass on its southern wall. An angled wall lends character to the kitchen/dining area. The master suite occupies the entire second level with its own bath, dressing area, walk-in closet, storage nook and private deck.

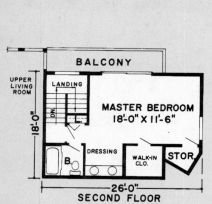

No. 10396

BALCONY

UPPER LIVING ROOM

LANDING

DN

MASTER BEDROOM
18'-0" X 11'-6"

B

DRESSING

WALK-IN CLO.

STOR.

18'-0"

26'-0"

SECOND FLOOR

Photography by John Ehrenclou

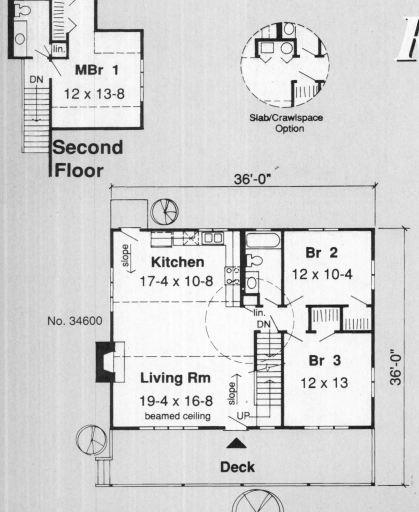

Second Floor

MBr 1
12 x 13-8

DN

lin.

Slab/Crawlspace
Option

No. 34600

36'-0"

slope

Kitchen
17-4 x 10-8

Br 2
12 x 10-4

lin.

DN

Br 3
12 x 13

Living Rm
19-4 x 16-8
beamed ceiling

slope

UP

36'-0"

Deck

First Floor

*R*ustic Exterior
Complete Home

No. 34600

Although rustic in appearance, the interior of this cabin is quiet, modern and comfortable. Small in overall size, it still contains three bedrooms and two baths in addition to a large, two-story living room with exposed beams. As a hunting/fishing lodge or mountain retreat, this compares well.

First floor — 1,013 sq. ft.
Second floor — 315 sq.ft.
Basement — 1,013 sq. ft.

Total living area —1,328 sq. ft.

Photography by Steele Photographers

Photography by American Wood Council

*C*omfortable Living...

No. 26760

*I*n A Unique
Design Package

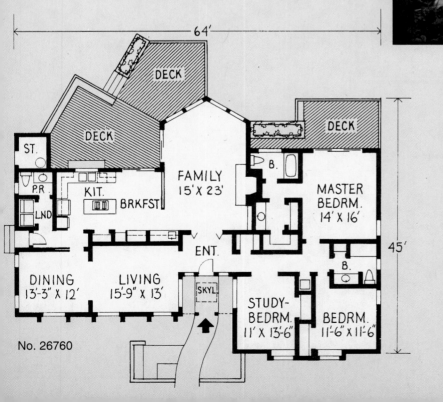

The central focus of this highly pleasing three bedroom ranch is the family room, its largest most architecturally interesting space. The first room seen upon entering, this room features a prow shape, a beamed ceiling and a fireplace. Sliding glass doors give access to the multi-leveled deck. The well designed kitchen has a center work island and a large breakfast area overlooking the deck. The dining room and the living room are conveniently placed for ease of entertaining. The master bedroom has a private bath and dressing room. Also included are plenty of closets and a private deck. Two smaller bedrooms share a spacious bath.

Main living area — 2,023 sq. ft.
Decks — 589 sq. ft.
Outdoor storage — 36 sq. ft.

Total living area — 2,023 sq. ft.

No. 26760

A Special Garden Delight

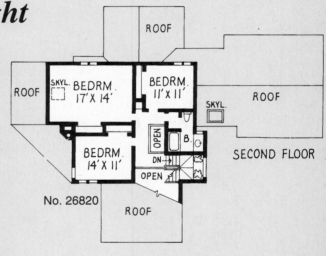

ROOF

ROOF

SKYL. BEDRM. 17' X 14'

BEDRM. 11' X 11'

SKYL.

ROOF

BEDRM. 14' X 11'

OPEN

B.

DN

OPEN

SECOND FLOOR

No. 26820

ROOF

Photography by American Wood Council

—72'—

DECK

MASTER BEDRM. 15' X 14'

KIT. 17' X 10'

B.

L.

GARAGE 22' X 24'

DINING 14' X 14'

P.R.

POTTING RM.

GARDEN RM.

KEEPING RM. 14' X 17'

ENT.

DN

DN UP

FIRST FLOOR

DECK

LIVING 18' X 14'

56'-6"

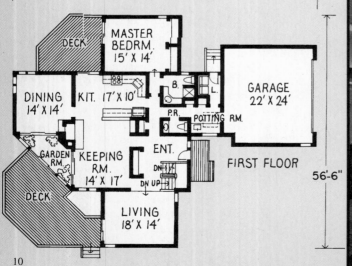

10

First level — 1,618 sq. ft.
Second level — 907 sq. ft.
Basement — 1,621 sq. ft.
Garage — 552 sq. ft.
Garden room — 98 sq. ft.

Total living area — 2,525 sq. ft.

One of the smallest rooms in this house might turn out to be the most important. The garden room, oriented south or southwest, uses its skylight and insulating glass wall not only to make plants thrive, but also to help heat the house. Sliding glass doors can be opened to draw this heat into the living areas to supplement the conventional mechanical system. The design guarantees many pleasures for outdoor enthusiasts: two decks, skylighting, year-round green views of the garden room, even a potting room by the back door. The core of the plan is a "keeping room" combining kitchen, breakfast area and family area by a fireplace. Each living area has three exposures for exhilarating light and summer comfort.

No. 26820

Photography by John Ehrenclou

Greenhouse Entrance
Accents Two-Story Berm

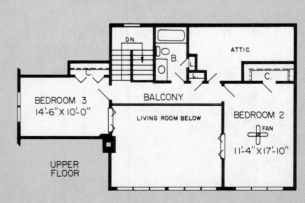

No. 10541

BEDROOM 3
14'-6"X10'-0"

DN.

C.

B.

ATTIC

C.

BALCONY

LIVING ROOM BELOW

BEDROOM 2

FAN

11'-4"X17'-10"

UPPER
FLOOR

Greenhouse entry into a spacious living area provides a bit of elegance as well as practicality for the energy-wise family. Both the living room and the master bedroom are furnished with ceiling fans and a heat-circulating stove. The second floor balcony, which connects bedrooms two and three upstairs, overlooks the living room. Two full baths and a powder room provide ample space for family and guests. Lots of closet space and a large utility room are features everyone appreciates.

Main floor — 1,474 sq. ft.
Upper floor — 1,044 sq. ft.
Garage — 616 sq. ft.

Total living area — 2,518 sq. ft.

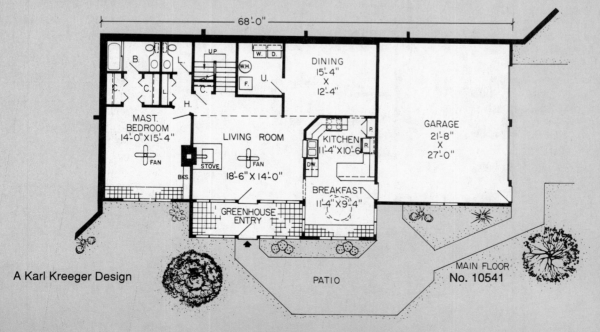

A Karl Kreeger Design

MAIN FLOOR
No. 10541

Photography by John Ehrenclou

C¹halet Beach Home Has Many Time-Saving Features

No. 10054

Perfect for vacation living, this chalet beach home features several work-saving ideas, including a breakfast bar which divides living room and kitchen. The ample living/dining room spills out onto the attractive 24 foot deck. Four closeted bedrooms include two upstairs, favored with balconies and reached by a spiral staircase off the living room. The home is built on treated pilings, but might also be constructed on a conventional foundation.

First floor — 768 sq. ft.
Second floor — 406 sq. ft.

Total living area — 1,174 sq. ft.

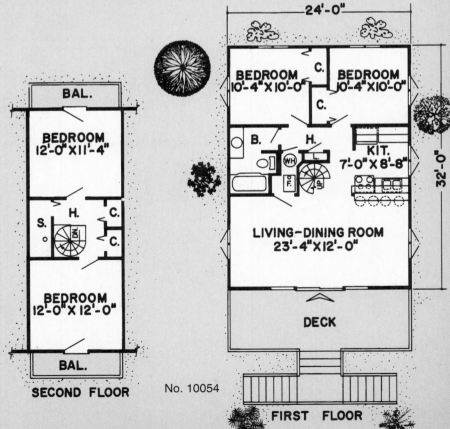

No. 10054

SECOND FLOOR

FIRST FLOOR

Photography by John Ehrenclou

*M*ulti-Level Contemporary Has Rustic Charm

The features of this multi-level Contemporary home lend character to both the exterior and interior. A wooden deck skirts most of three sides. The variety in the size and shape of doors and windows adds charm. Inside, the living room forms a unique living center. It can be reached from sliding glass doors from the deck or down several steps from the main living level inside. It is overlooked by a low balcony from the entryway and dining room on the lower level and from the second floor landing. Large windows on both the right and the left keep it well lit. Ceilings slope upward two stories. A partial basement is located below the design.

First floor — 769 sq. ft.
Second floor — 572 sq. ft.
Basement — 546 sq. ft.

Total living area — 1,341 sq. ft.

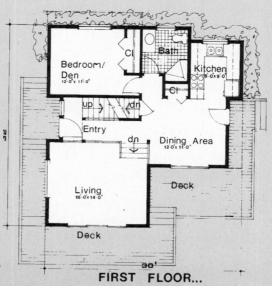

No. 26111

Bedroom/ Den
12'-0"x 11'-0"

Bath

Cl

Kitchen
8'-0"x 9'-0"

Cl

up
dn

Entry

dn

Dining Area
12'-0"x 11'-0"

Living
16'-0"x 14'-0"

Deck

Deck

30'

FIRST FLOOR...

Bedroom
12'-0"x 13'-0"

Cl

Bath

Cl

Skylights

dn

Bedroom
12'-0"x 20'-0"

Balcony

Open to Living

Cl

30'

SECOND FLOOR...

No. 26111

No. 19391

Photography by William Smith Photographers

*V*acation Haven

This house has a very unique design which can be built on lots of different sites. The main floor has a large living room with a built-in fireplace which flows into a private sun porch. The dining room has a bar and is included in the spacious back deck. The kitchen flows into a breakfast nook which is bright and sunny. A laundry room, full bath and three-car garage are also on the first floor. The second floor has a family room with an old-fashioned wood stove, a cedar closet and a bedroom with a bath. The master bedroom suite includes a sun deck, huge closets, a large bathroom and a fireplace. The third floor includes a spiral staircase to the cupola, a loft, an office with two skylights and a deck.

First floor — 1,246 sq. ft.
Second floor — 1,533 sq. ft.
Loft — 557 sq. ft.
Basement — 1,390 sq. ft.
Garage — 766 sq. ft.

Total living area — 3,336 sq. ft.

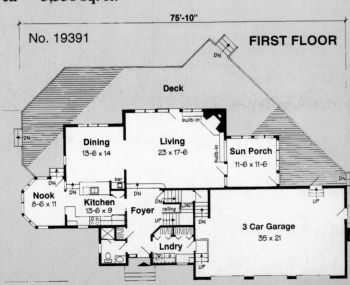

*E*asy and Complete Living On One Level

No. 24311

Family vacations are memories in the making. This home will help to make those precious times. Three bedrooms give private space to all. Don't have a large family, make one bedroom into a study or maybe a hobby room, the possibilities are yours. The living room has a fireplace and is large and open and can extend your living area out of the home with access to two decks. The efficient kitchen opens to the dining area. The master bedroom features a private bath with corner tub. There are also two closets in this room. Looking forward to retirement? This home may be what you are looking for. All the living area is on one floor yet it is spacious and it is layed out with convenience in mind.

Main living area — 1,136 sq. ft.

Total living area — 1,136 sq. ft.

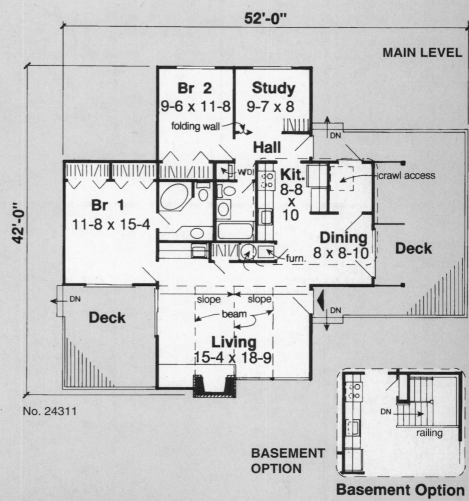

MAIN LEVEL

52'-0"

42'-0"

Br 2
9-6 x 11-8
folding wall

Study
9-7 x 8

DN

Hall

W D

Kit.
8-8 x 10

crawl access

Br 1
11-8 x 15-4

furn.

Dining
8 x 8-10

Deck

DN
Deck

slope   slope
beam

DN

Living
15-4 x 18-9

No. 24311

BASEMENT OPTION

DN
railing

Basement Option

Simple Lines Enhanced by Elegant Window Treatment

No. 34150

Consider this plan if you work at home and would enjoy a homey, well lit office or den. The huge, arched window floods the front room with light. This house offers a lot of other practical details for the two-career family. Compact and efficient use of space means less to clean and organize. Yet the open plan keeps the home from feeling too small and cramped. Other features like plenty of closet space, step-saving laundry facilities, easily-cleaned kitchen, and a window wall in the living room make this a delightful plan.

Main living area — 1,486 sq. ft.
Garage — 462 sq. ft.
Basement — 1,486 sq. ft.

Total living area — 1,486 sq. ft.

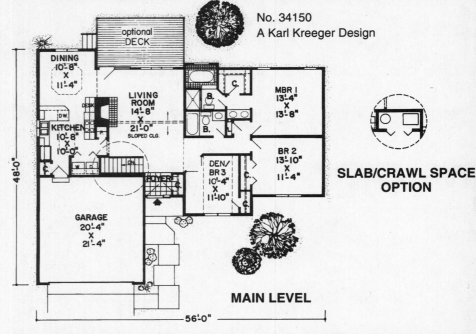

No. 34150
A Karl Kreeger Design

SLAB/CRAWL SPACE OPTION

MAIN LEVEL

Vacation Retreat Suits Year-round Living

No. 1078

A long central hallway divides formal from informal areas, assuring privacy for the two bedrooms located in the rear. Also located along the central portion of the design are a utility room and a neighboring bath. The furnace, water heater and washer/dryer units are housed in the utility room. An open living/dining room area with exposed beams, sloping ceilings and optional fireplace occupies the front. Two pairs of sliding glass doors access the large deck from this area. The house may also be entered from the carport on the right or the deck on the left.

First floor — 1,024 sq. ft.
Carport & storage — 387 sq. ft.
Deck — 411 sq. ft.

Total living area — 1,024 sq. ft.

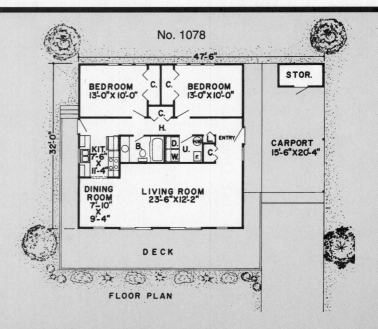

No. 1078

FLOOR PLAN

Excellent Choice for Sloping Lots

No. 9714

With its sloping, striking design, this split-foyer plan combines outdoor living areas and a highly livable lower level. Facing the front and opening to the terrace, the family room dominates the lower level, which also includes a bedroom, a hobby room, and a full bath with shower. Above, a sun deck greets the living room and dining room. A tiled country kitchen, complete with a cooking island and built-in laundry, three bedrooms and two full baths comprise the sleeping wing.

Main level — 1,748 sq. ft.
Lower level — 932 sq. ft.
Garage — 768 sq. ft.

Total living area — 2,680 sq. ft.

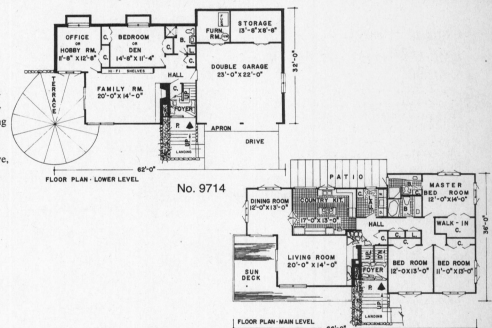

No. 9714

FLOOR PLAN · LOWER LEVEL

FLOOR PLAN · MAIN LEVEL

Central Courtyard Features Pool

No. 10507

Created for gracious living, this design is organized around a central courtyard complete with pool. Secluded near one corner of the courtyard, the master bedroom suite is accented by a skylight, spacious walk-in closet, and a bath which accommodates swimmers and sunbathers. The living room, dining room and kitchen occupy another corner. The well-placed kitchen easily serves the patio for comfortable outdoor entertaining. A family room and two more bedrooms complete the design.

Main living area — 2,194 sq. ft.
Garage — 576 sq. ft.

Total living area — 2,194 sq. ft.

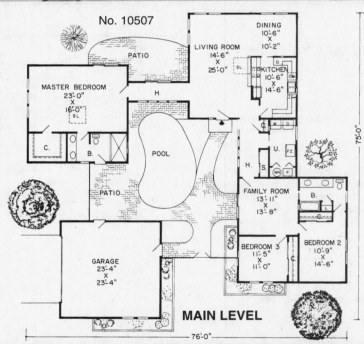

Deck Encircles Compact Home

No. 19709

Suitable for either a vacation home or a small family residence, this modest two bedroom home provides a spacious living area and a comfortable deck for outdoor relaxation. The free flow of space in the dining area, living area, and kitchen make the areas seem larger. Two sets of sliding glass doors provide light and access to the deck. The kitchen pantry is a welcome bonus.

Main living area — 792 sq. ft.
Deck — 588 sq. ft.

Total living area — 792 sq. ft.

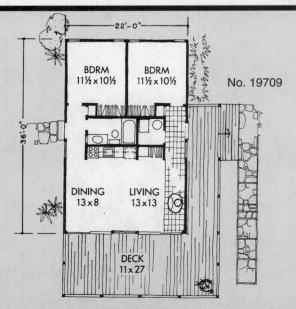

FLOOR PLAN

Design Features Six Ideas

No. 1074

Simple lines flow from this six-sided design. It's affordably scaled, but sizable enough for a growing family. Active living areas are snuggled centrally between two quiet bedroom and bath areas in the floor plan. A small hallway, leading to two bedrooms and a full bath on the right side, may be completely shut off from the living room, providing seclusion. Another bath lies behind a third bedroom on the left side, complete with washer/dryer facilities and close enough to a stoop and rear entrance to serve as a mudroom.

Main living area — 1,040 sq. ft.
Storage — 44 sq. ft.
Deck — 258 sq. ft.
Carport — 230 sq. ft.

Total living area — 1,040 sq. ft.

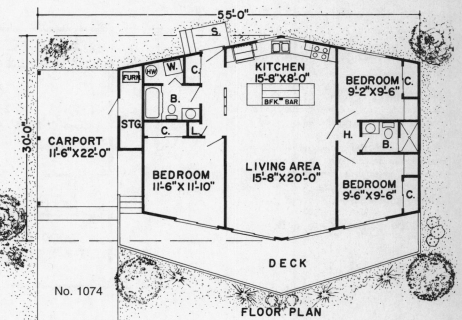

CARPORT
11'-6"X22'-0"

STG.

FURN HW W. C.

B.
C. L.

BEDROOM
11'-6"X 11'-10"

KITCHEN
15'-8"X8'-0"
BFK. BAR

LIVING AREA
15'-8"X20'-0"

S.

BEDROOM C.
9'-2"X9'-6"

H. B.

BEDROOM
9'-6"X9'-6" C.

55'-0"

30'-0"

DECK

No. 1074

FLOOR PLAN

Deck Enlarges, Enhances Cottage

No. 10306

Ideal for a beach or mountain vacation home, this one bedroom cottage supplies a large wood deck for dining, sunbathing, or relaxing with friends. The plan is strictly functional and calls for an 11 foot bedroom with a shower and a simple, one wall kitchen open to the living room. Two smaller decks are also shown.

Main living area — 408 sq. ft.

Total living area — 408 sq. ft.

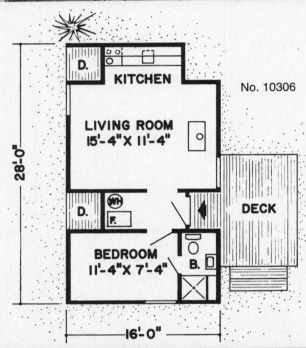

No. 10306

KITCHEN

LIVING ROOM
15'-4" X 11'-4"

DECK

BEDROOM
11'-4" X 7'-4"

28'-0"

16'-0"

Designed for Relaxed Living

No. 26070

Both the exterior and interior design of this plan speak of relaxed living. A delightful feeling of flowing space is created by four levels. The master bedroom has a level of its own for complete privacy as does the guest bedroom. A balcony off the master bedroom looks out onto the lower living area, where you can relax before the fireplace or step out onto the patio. Up seven steps from the living area you'll find yourself on the kitchen/dining level. A storage/laundry area and sauna are in a building of their own separated from the rest of the house by a drive-thru. Three complete baths finish out the interior floor plan.

Middle & Upper levels — 797 sq. ft.
Lower level — 1,133 sq. ft.
Storage, laundry & sauna — 288 sq. ft.
Basement — 874 sq. ft.

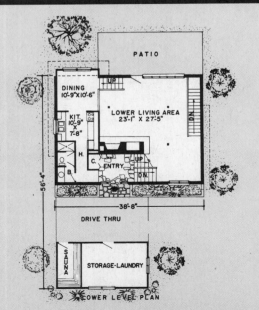

PATIO

DINING
10'-9" X 10'-6"

LOWER LIVING AREA
23'-1" X 27'-5"

KIT.
10'-9" X 7'-8"

ENTRY

56'-4"

38'-8"

DRIVE THRU

SAUNA

STORAGE-LAUNDRY

LOWER LEVEL PLAN

No. 26070

MASTER BEDROOM
15'-5" X 15'-10"

OPEN TO LIVING AREA

RAILING

GUEST BEDROOM
10'-1" X 16'-0"

DRESSING

BALCONY

CLO.

34'-0"

42'-0"

MIDDLE & UPPER LEVEL PLAN

Total living area — 1,930 sq. ft.

A-frame Can Be Built Quickly

No. 7664

Easy to apply, red cedar shake shingles are specified for the roof of this A-frame cabin and help make building-it-yourself a feasible and rewarding project. Constructed on a concrete slab, the cabin exudes relaxed informality through the warm natural tones of exposed beams and unfinished wood interior.

Main floor — 560 sq. ft.
Upper level — 240 sq. ft.

Total living area — 800 sq. ft.

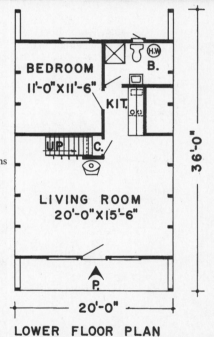

LOWER FLOOR PLAN

BEDROOM
11'-0"x11'-6"

B.

KIT.

UP. C.

LIVING ROOM
20'-0"x15'-6"

P.

36'-0"

20'-0"

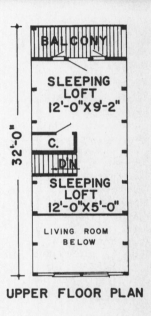

UPPER FLOOR PLAN

No. 7664

BALCONY

SLEEPING LOFT
12'-0"x9'-2"

C.

DN.

SLEEPING LOFT
12'-0"x5'-0"

LIVING ROOM BELOW

32'-0"

Living Room Focus of Spacious Home

No. 10328

Equipped with fireplace and sliding glass doors to the bordering deck, the two-story living room creates a sizeable and airy center for family activity. A well-planned traffic pattern connects the dining area, kitchen, laundry niche and bath. Closets are plentiful, and a total of three 15-foot bedrooms are shown. A balcony overlooking the open living room is featured on the second floor.

First floor — 1,024 sq. ft.
Second floor — 576 sq. ft.
Basement — 1,024 sq. ft.

Total living area — 1,600 sq. ft.

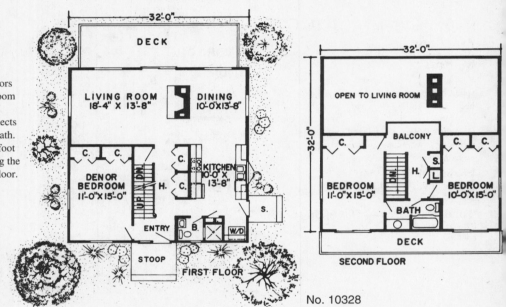

No. 10328

Singular Home is Practical to Build

No. 9950

Distinctive as this home may appear, with its deck-encircled hexagonal living room, its construction is actually quite practical. The main level houses the living room, which exhibits exposed beams and a cathedral ceiling, four bedrooms, two baths, a dining room and a kitchen. On the lower level, an enormous family room opens to a patio, with a built-in barbecue. Another bedroom, den and bath with a shower are detailed. Boat storage is also provided on this level.

First floor — 1,672 sq. ft.
Lower floor — 1,672 sq. ft.
Garage — 484 sq. ft.

Total living area — 3,344 sq. ft.

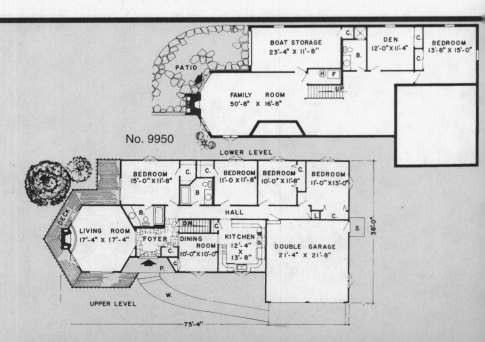

No. 9950

Sun Deck, Covered Patio Invite Outdoor Living

No. 9840

Encircling part of three sides of this home, an expansive sun deck spills off the living room and allows an unparalleled view of lake or mountain surroundings. Beneath the sun deck, a stone patio balances the stone siding of the family room and is reached via sliding glass doors. The first level also includes a large hobby room, utility and storage room, and half bath. Two bedrooms, a full bath, and kitchen with breakfast bar complete the upstairs plan, and a substantial sleeping loft with closet comprises the third level.

First floor — 1,120 sq. ft.
Lower level — 1,120 sq. ft.
Upper level — 340 sq. ft.

Total living area — 2,580 sq. ft.

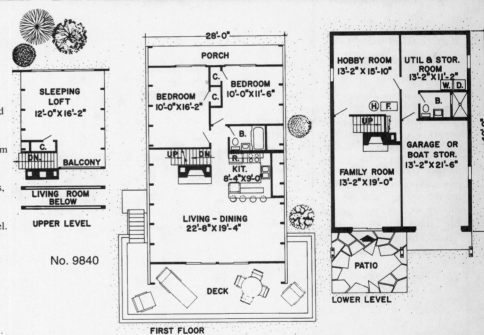

SLEEPING LOFT
12'-0" X 16'-2"

DN. C.

BALCONY

LIVING ROOM BELOW

UPPER LEVEL

No. 9840

28'-0"

PORCH

C.

BEDROOM 10'-0" X 16'-2"

C.

BEDROOM 10'-0" X 11'-6"

B.

UP DN

R.

KIT. 8'-4" X 9'-0"

LIVING - DINING 22'-8" X 19'-4"

DECK

FIRST FLOOR

HOBBY ROOM 13'-2" X 15'-10"

UTIL & STOR. ROOM 13'-2" X 11'-2"

W. D.

H. F.

UP

B.

FAMILY ROOM 13'-2" X 19'-0"

GARAGE OR BOAT STOR. 13'-2" X 21'-6"

40'-0"

PATIO

LOWER LEVEL

Recreation Room Welcomes You

No. 9964

This romantic chalet design would be equally appealing along an ocean beach or mountain stream. Restful log fires will add atmosphere in the sizable recreation room bordering the patio of this chalet. Upstairs, another fireplace warms the living and dining rooms which are accessible to the large wooden sun deck. Four bedrooms and two baths are outlined. The home is completely insulated for year round convenience and contains washer and dryer space.

First floor — 896 sq. ft.
Second floor — 457 sq. ft.
Basement — 864 sq. ft.

Total living area — 1,353 sq. ft.

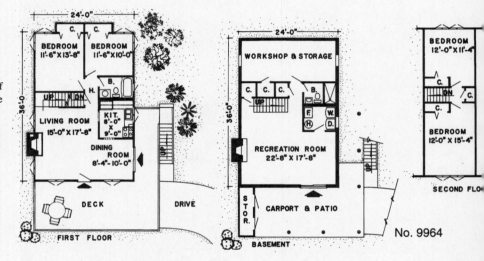

Delightful, Compact Home

No. 34003

Hanging plants would make for a magnificent entrance to this charming home. Walk into the fireplaced living room brightened by a wonderful picture window. The kitchen and dining area are separated by a counter island featuring double sinks. In the hallway, toward the bedrooms, is a linen closet and full bath. The master bedroom features its own private bath and double closets. The two other bedrooms have good-sized closets, keeping clutter to a minimum. Many windows throughout this home lighten up each room, creating a warm cozy atmosphere. Please indicate slab, crawl space or basement foundation when ordering.

Main living area — 1,146 sq. ft.

Total living area — 1,146 sq. ft.

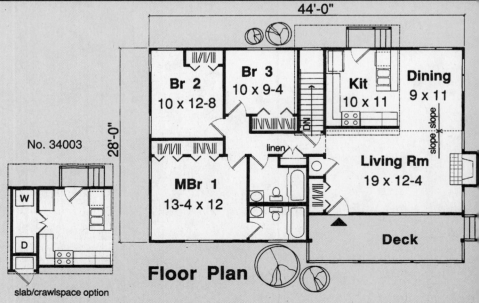

Double-Closeted Bedrooms Highlight Plan

No. 10234

Generously proportioned bedrooms, with double closets and bordering laundry and full bath, promise livability in this trim leisure plan. For entertaining, the 22 foot living room expands via two sets of sliding glass doors to the large balcony. A spacious kitchen offers dining space and a pantry and opens to the wooden deck for easily prepared outdoor meals. The lower level has a garage, workbench, and storage for camper or trailer.

Upper level — 1,254 sq. ft.
Lower level — 1,064 sq. ft.

Total living area — 2,318 sq. ft.

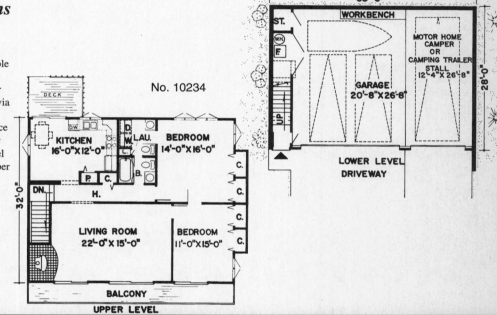

No. 10234

DECK

KITCHEN 16'-0" X 12'-0"

W LAU.

BEDROOM 14'-0" X 16'-0"

P. C. B.

DN.

H.

LIVING ROOM 22'-0" X 15'-0"

BEDROOM 11'-0" X 15'-0"

C. C. C. C.

32'-0"

BALCONY

UPPER LEVEL

38'-0"

ST.

WH F

WORKBENCH

MOTOR HOME CAMPER OR CAMPING TRAILER STALL 12'-4" X 26'-8"

GARAGE 20'-8" X 26'-8"

UP

28'-0"

LOWER LEVEL DRIVEWAY

Lakeshore Home Spells Livable

No. 10138

Take the luxurious features of a second floor sundeck, ground level patio, and spacious living and family rooms; combine with four full size bedrooms; add to this two and one-half baths in a unique and practical arrangement, a ground-floor utility room and a well-grouped kitchen, and you've got a home that's both livable and dazzling.

Upper level — 1,196 sq. ft.
Lower level — 1,196 sq. ft.

Total living area — 2,392 sq. ft.

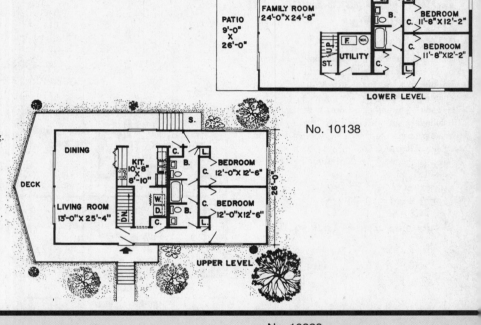

No. 10138

Excellent Zoning Marks A-frame

No. 10228

In addition to separating bedrooms and living area by placing them on different floors, this rustic A-frame plan also uses the entry and half bath to divide the family-kitchen and adjoining patio from the guest-oriented living room. A dining space overlooks the patio through sliding glass doors. Upstairs, two spacious bedrooms are served by private decks, a full bath, and a linen closet.

First floor — 768 sq. ft.
Second floor — 521 sq. ft.

Total living area — 1,289 sq. ft.

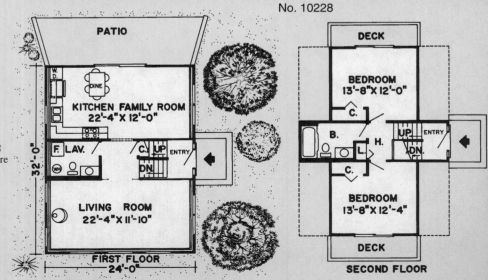

No. 10228

Compact Design Promotes Leisure

No. 10518

Built to be efficient, this home still has lots of living space in a three bedroom, two bath design. The trim on the deck suggests a chalet, but this modern home would be welcome anywhere. Tucked into the peak of the roof is the master bedroom with its own private bath. Two more bedrooms plus a four-piece bath are located on the first floor. The combined living/dining room opens onto the deck which extends the full width of the house. The front kitchen is easily accessible from the entry and is designed for efficient meal preparation.

First floor — 864 sq. ft.
Second floor — 307 sq. ft.

Total living area — 1,171 sq. ft.

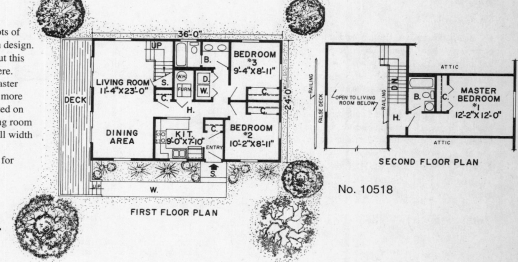

FIRST FLOOR PLAN

SECOND FLOOR PLAN

No. 10518

Bedrooms Enjoy Access to Deck

No. 10220

To encourage a relaxed lifestyle and enjoyment of the outdoors, a 50 foot wooden deck fronts this vacation retreat and opens to two bedrooms as well as the living area. Complete but simple, the plan offers a living area with two closets and a prefab fireplace, open to a compact kitchen with rear entrance. The separate laundry room also houses the furnace and water heater, and the large bath features double sinks. The plan can be built without one or both bedrooms if desired.

Family area — 576 sq. ft.
Bedroom 1 — 168 sq. ft.
Bedroom 2 — 144 sq. ft.

Total living area — 888 sq. ft.

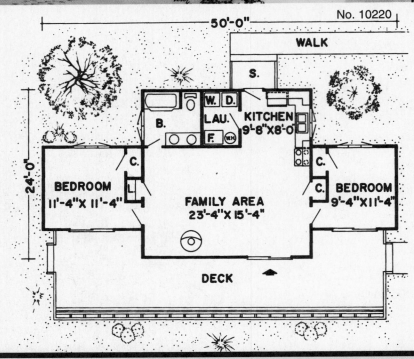

Deck Defies Gravity

No. 24306

This contemporary home is perfect for a mountainside with a far-reaching view. Imagine sitting by the fireplace in this large sunny living room and gazing into the distance. The spiral staircase adds a bit of style to this open plan. The galley kitchen has access to the rear deck and lies next to two bedrooms and a full bath with a convenient linen closet. The second floor has a loft, a roomy studio, a third bedroom with its own deck and a bathroom.

First floor — 841 sq. ft.
Second floor — 489 sq. ft.

Total living area — 1,330 sq. ft.

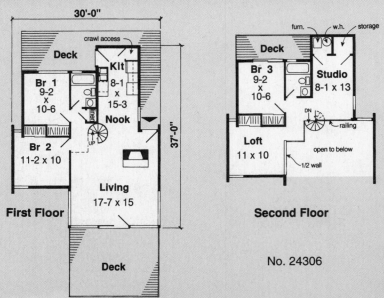

Home on a Hill

No. 20501

Your hillside lot is no problem if you choose this spectacular, multi-level sun-catcher. Window walls combine with sliders to unite active areas with a huge outdoor deck. Interior spaces flow together for an open feeling that's accentuated by the sloping ceilings and towering fireplace in the living room. Thanks to the island kitchen, even the cook can stay involved in the action. Walk up a short flight to reach the laundry room, a full bath, and two bedrooms, each with a walk-in closet. Up a separate staircase, you'll find the master suite, truly a private retreat complete with a garden spa, abundant closets, and balcony.

First floor — 1,316 sq. ft.
Second floor — 592 sq. ft.

Total living area — 1,908 sq. ft.

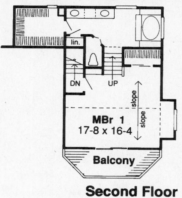

Second Floor

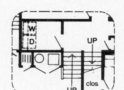

Pier/Crawl Space Opt.

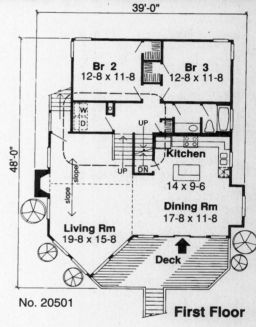

No. 20501   **First Floor**

No. 24319

*H*ome With Many Views

This home is a vacation haven with views from every room whether it is situated on a lake or a mountaintop. The main floor features a living room and dining room split by a fireplace. The kitchen flows into the dining room and is gracefully separated by a bar. There is a bedroom and a full bath on the main floor. The second floor has a bedroom or library loft, with clerestory windows, which opens above the living room. The master bedroom and bath are also on the top floor. The lower floor has a large recreation room with a whirlpool tub and a bar, a laundry room and a garage. This home has large decks and windows on one entire side.

Main floor — 720 sq. ft.
Upper floor — 563 sq. ft.
Lower floor — 377 sq. ft.
Garage — 240 sq. ft.

Total living area — 1,660 sq. ft.

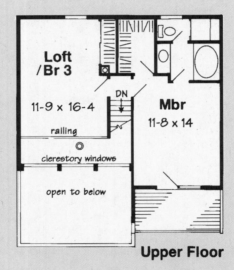

No. 24319

Upper Floor

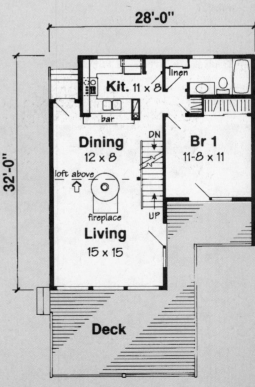

Main Floor

Compact Contemporary

No. 91002

Here's a beautiful little dream house with your budget in mind. With soaring ceilings and dramatic window treatments, you'll enjoy solar savings and delightful views from all the main living areas and sleeping loft. The main floor location of the bedroom and full bath makes one floor living simple. But, with a half-bath, sleeping room and loft upstairs, there's room for more.

First floor — 744 sq. ft.
Second floor — 288 sq. ft.

Total living area — 1,032 sq. ft.

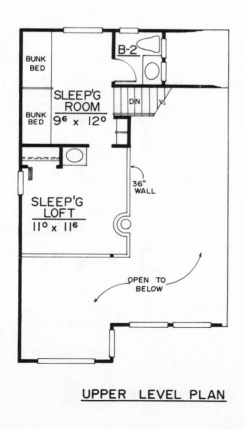

UPPER LEVEL PLAN

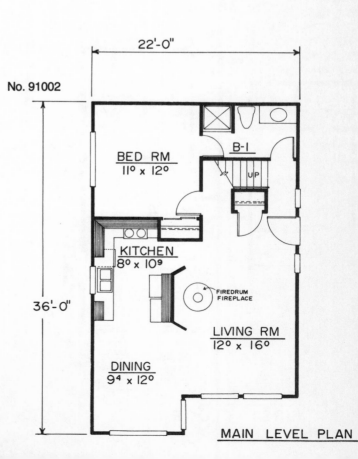

MAIN LEVEL PLAN

Contemporary Design Features Sunken Living Room

No. 26112

Wood adds its warmth to the contemporary features of this passive solar design. Generous use of southern glass doors and windows, an air lock entry, skylights and a living room fireplace reduce energy needs. R-26 insulation is used for floors and sloping ceilings. Decking rims the front of the home and gives access through sliding glass doors to a bedroom-den area and living room. The dining room lies up several steps from the living room and is separated from it by a half wall. The dining room flows into the kitchen through an eating bar. A second floor landing balcony overlooks the living room. Two bedrooms, one with its own private deck, and a full bath finish the second level.

First floor — 911 sq. ft.
Second floor — 576 sq. ft.
Basement — 911 sq. ft.

Total living area — 1,487 sq. ft.

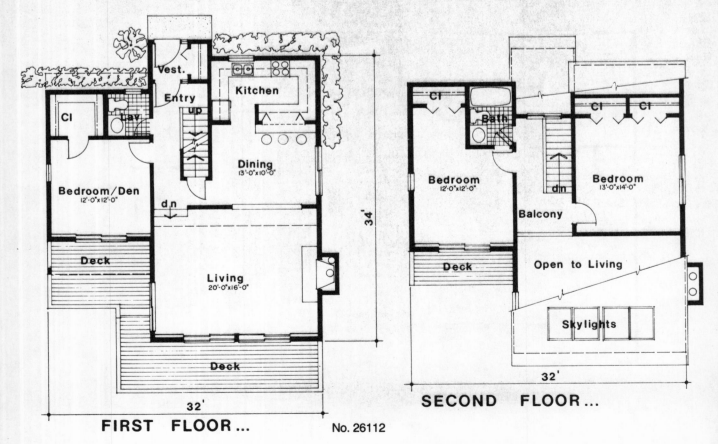

FIRST FLOOR ...   No. 26112

SECOND FLOOR ...

Old-American Saltbox Design

No. 90123

A sloping living room ceiling lends a sense of spaciousness to the modest square footage. You can relax in front of the centrally located fireplace in cool weather or move through triple sliding glass doors to the roomy deck when the weather is warmer. Behind the living room lies a bedroom, full bath and the kitchen/dining area which has a window seat. Laundry facilities are conveniently placed off the kitchen. On the left of the living room a quiet corner has been tucked under the stairs leading to the second floor. The second level affords two equal-sized bedrooms (one with its own private deck), joined by a full bath. This plan can be built with a slab foundation only.

First floor — 840 sq. ft.
Second floor — 440 sq. ft.

Total living area — 1,280 sq. ft.

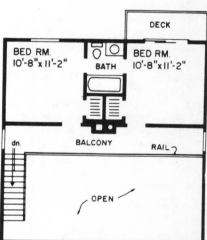

SECOND FLOOR

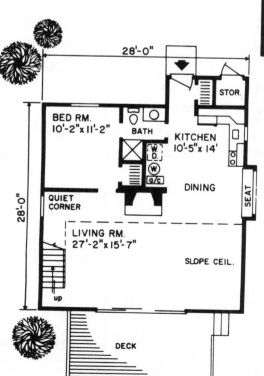

No. 90123

FIRST FLOOR

No Wasted Space

No. 90412

The open floor plan of this modified A-frame design virtually eliminates wasted hall space. The centrally located Great room features a cathedral ceiling with exposed wood beams and large areas of fixed glass on both front and rear. Living and dining areas are virtually separated by a massive stone fireplace. The isolated master suite features a walk-in closet and sliding glass doors opening onto the front deck. A walk-thru utility room provides easy access from the carport and outside storage areas to the compact kitchen. On the opposite side of the Great room are two additional bedrooms and a second full bath. A full length deck and vertical wood siding with stone accents on the corners provide a rustic yet contemporary exterior. Specify crawlspace, basement or slab foundation when ordering.

Main living area — 1,454 sq. ft.

Total living area — 1,454 sq. ft.

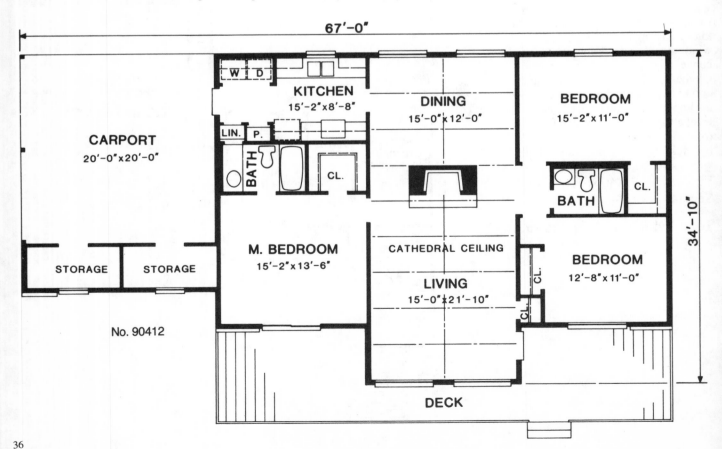

No. 90412

Rear of Home as Attractive as Front

No. 90413

The rear of this contemporary home features a massive stone fireplace and a full length deck which make it ideal for a mountain, golf course, lake, or other location where both the front and rear are visible. Sliding glass doors in the family room and breakfast nook open onto the deck. The modified A-frame design combines a cathedral ceiling over the sunken family room with a large studio over the two front bedrooms. An isolated master suite features a walk-in closet and compartmentalized bath with double vanity and linen closet. The front bedrooms include ample closet space and share a unique bath-and-a-half arrangement. On one side of the U-shaped kitchen and breakfast nook is the formal dining room which opens onto the foyer. On the other side is a utility room which can be entered from either the kitchen or garage. The exterior features a massive stone fireplace, large glass areas, and a combination of vertical wood siding and stone. This plan is available with a basement, slab or crawl space foundation. Please specify when ordering.

First floor — 2,192 sq. ft.
Second floor — 248 sq. ft.
Basement — 2,192 sq. ft.

Total living area — 2,440 sq. ft.

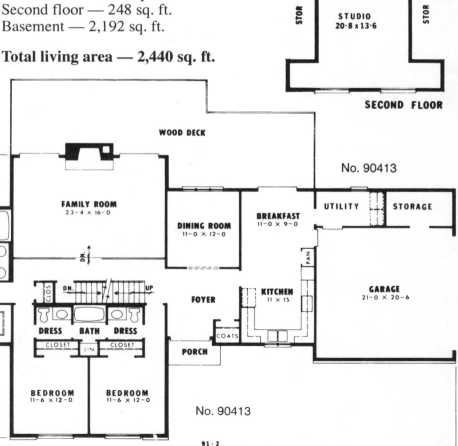

Compact Home for a Small Space

No. 90500

A massive bay window is the dominant feature in the facade of this cozy home with attached two-car garage. From the entry, there are three ways to walk. Turn left into the fireplaced living room and adjoining dining room. Or walk straight into the kitchen and breakfast nook, which extends to a covered porch. Step down the hall on the right to the master suite, full bath, and a second bedroom. The TV room, which can double as a third bedroom, completes the circlular floor plan in this convenient, one-level abode.

Main living area — 1,299 sq. ft.
Garage — 2-car

Total living area — 1,299 sq. ft.

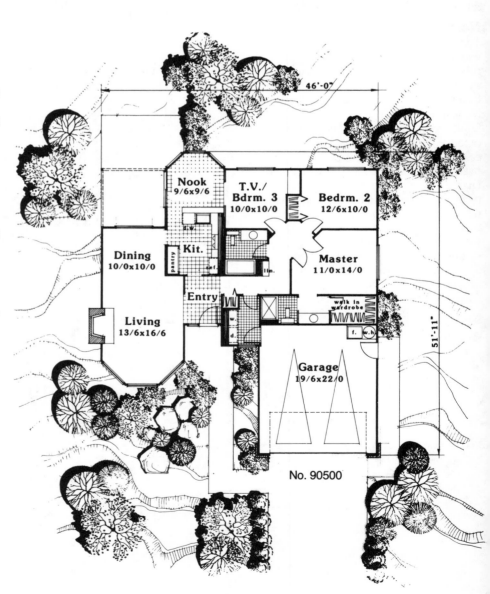

Nook
9/6x9/6

T.V./
Bdrm. 3
10/0x10/0

Bedrm. 2
12/6x10/0

Dining
10/0x10/0

Kit.

Master
11/0x14/0

Entry

walk in
wardrobe

Living
13/6x16/6

Garage
19/6x22/0

46'-0"

51'-11"

No. 90500

Call This Home

No. 90424

With a covered porch in the front and a screened porch in back, this traditional farmhouse has all the amenities. The great room, with its stone fireplace, occupies the center of this home and has direct access to the screened porch. To the right lies the island kitchen, dining room and bayed breakfast room and to the left is the secluded master bedroom with its five-piece bath and his and hers walk-in closets. Upstairs lies two more bedrooms, each with plenty of closet space and private access to the shared bath.

First floor — 1,535 sq. ft.
Second floor — 765 sq. ft.
Garage — 2-car
Basement — 1,091 sq. ft.

Total living area — 2,300 sq. ft.

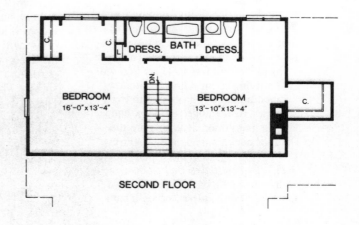

C.
DRESS. BATH DRESS.
C.
DN.
BEDROOM
16'-0" x 13'-4"
BEDROOM
13'-10" x 13'-4"
C.

SECOND FLOOR

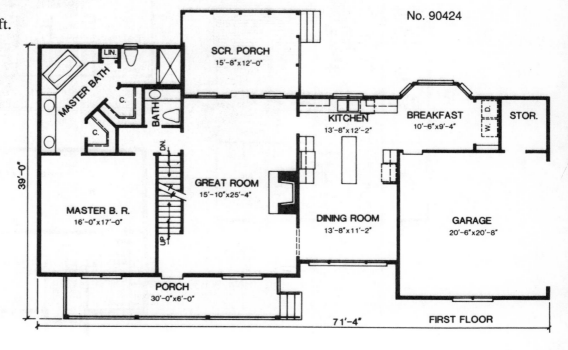

No. 90424

SCR. PORCH
15'-8" x 12'-0"

MASTER BATH
LIN.
C.
BATH
C.

KITCHEN
13'-8" x 12'-2"
BREAKFAST
10'-6" x 9'-4"
W. D.
STOR.

DN.
GREAT ROOM
15'-10" x 25'-4"

MASTER B. R.
16'-0" x 17'-0"

UP

DINING ROOM
13'-8" x 11'-2"

GARAGE
20'-6" x 20'-8"

39'-0"

PORCH
30'-0" x 6'-0"

71'-4"

FIRST FLOOR

A House that Fits

No. 90636

Natural exterior siding, sloping roofs, decks and large windows make this house attractive for most settings. A protected main entrance leads up four steps to the first floor. There you will find a living room with a ceiling that slants dramatically from one to two stories, a rustic stone fireplace, and sliding glass doors leading onto the outdoor deck. An adjacent, roomy kitchen/dining room also opens to the deck. There are two first floor bedrooms and a bath. Upstairs, two more bedrooms, separated by a bath, open onto an exterior balcony. The clerestory windows in the hall shed light on an interior balcony that the kids will love. Wherever it is built, this house will belong. This plan is available with a partial basement or partial crawl space foundation. Please specify when ordering.

First floor — 928 sq. ft.
Second floor — 468 sq. ft.

Total living area — 1,396 sq. ft.

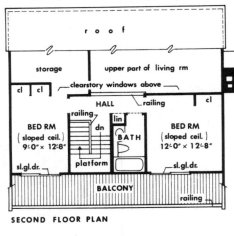

SECOND FLOOR PLAN

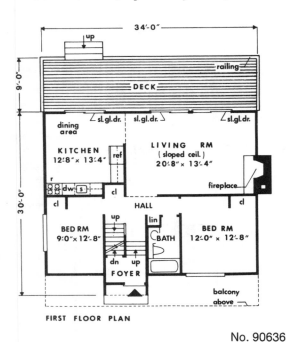

FIRST FLOOR PLAN

No. 90636

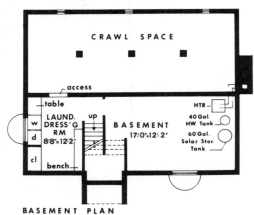

BASEMENT PLAN

Rustic Vacation House

No. 90004

This compact three-bedroom cabin, designed for vacations and late retirement, would suit many areas. The stone and wood exterior requires little maintenance. Two porches and an outdoor balcony make the most of entertaining, relaxing, or just enjoying a sunset. From the foyer you can see the spiral stairway which leads to a balcony and an upstairs bedroom or studio. A wood fire always seems to make a house warmer and cozier, and this design includes a massive stone fireplace in the living room. The living room also has a pair of floor-to-ceiling windows at the gable end and sliding glass doors to a rear porch. There is a pantry adjoining the eat-in kitchen which has a small bay window over the sink. Off the foyer is a powder room. The design also includes two bedrooms and a bath on the first floor.

First floor — 1,020 sq. ft.
Second floor — 265 sq. ft.

Total living area — 1,285 sq. ft.

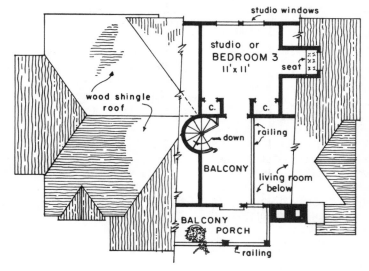

balcony level

No. 90004

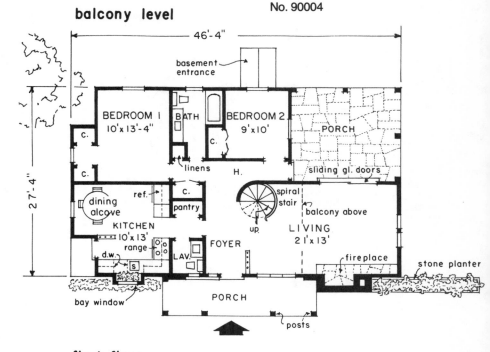

first floor

Secluded Vacation Retreat

No. 91704

The interior space design of this plan makes it quite suitable as a vacation home. A bedroom wing extends on either side of the high vaulted-living area, and offers extensive privacy. The two bedrooms on the main level are large, with 10-foot closets, and each has its own personal bath, double vanity and secluded patio, which is protected by the extended walls of the main living area. The living room is generous, with a large masonry fireplace and a circular stairway dominating the center of the house. One wall features windows along its full cathedral height. The kitchen has lots of counter space and cupboards, including a sink and chopping block island. The circular stairway leads to a loft room above. This could be a library, a guest bedroom, or a third bedroom. From this room, windowed doors open to a deck that is also the roof for the carport below.

First floor — 1,448 sq. ft.
Loft plan — 389 sq. ft.
Carport — 312 sq. ft.

Total living area — 1,837 sq. ft.

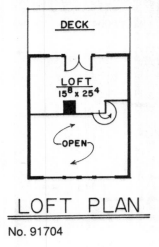

LOFT PLAN

No. 91704

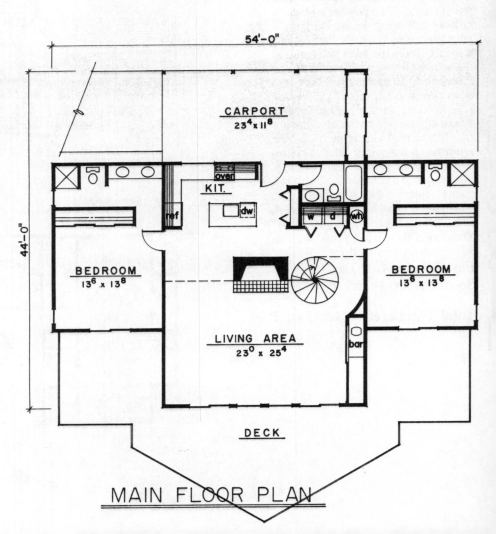

MAIN FLOOR PLAN

Neat and Tidy

No. 91033

This compact house has plenty of closets and storage areas where you can stow away the gear you usually need on vacation. The utility room is also larger than most, and opens directly outside, so there's no reason for anyone to track snow or mud in. Sliding glass doors lead from the two-story living room and dining room onto a paved patio. Tucked into a corner, the kitchen is both out of the way and convenient. A handsome stone fireplace adds a functional and decorative element to both the interior and exterior of the home. A downstairs bedroom will sleep either children or guests. Beyond the railed loft, a master suite with full bath and walk-in closet provides the owner of this home with every comfort. This plan is availabe with a basement or crawl space foundation. Please specify when ordering.

Main floor — 952 sq. ft.
Upper floor — 297 sq. ft.

Total living area — 1,249 sq. ft.

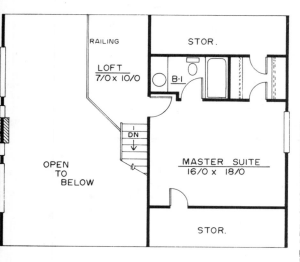

UPPER FLOOR

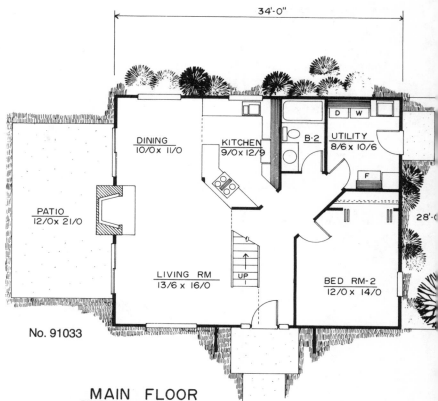

No. 91033

MAIN FLOOR

All You Need Is The Sea Breeze

No. 92800

This home, specifically designed for a coastal vista, boasts decks, screened in porch and windows that insure your taking advantage of your surroundings. You can enter the home into either the kitchen or through the screened in porch. The modern kitchen has the conveniences you're looking for with ample counter and cabinet space. The dining room and the living room lead into each other. This area of the house will enjoy the sea breezes and cross ventilation. There is even a fireplace for the cooler evenings, adding warmth and atmosphere to the room. One bedroom is on the first floor and two others are on the second floor. Layed out in this manner, the parents may have privacy while the children have their own living space. The wrap-around deck gives you one more place to enjoy the sun and the surf.

First floor — 900 sq. ft.
Second floor — 500 sq. ft.

Total living area — 1,400 sq. ft.

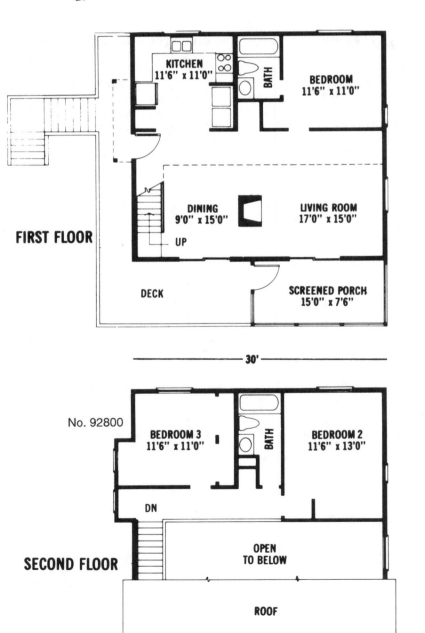

Lattice Trim Adds Nostalgic Charm

No. 99315

Thanks to vaulted ceilings and an ingenious plan, this wood and fieldstone classic feels much larger than its compact size. The entry, dominated by a skylit staircase to the bedroom floor, opens to the vaulted living room with a balcony view and floor-to-ceiling corner window treatment. Eat in the spacious, formal dining room, in the sunny breakfast nook off the kitchen, or, when the weather's nice, out on the adjoining deck. Pass-through convenience makes meal service easy wherever you choose to dine. A full bath at the top of the stairs serves the kids' bedrooms off the balcony hall. The master suite boasts its own, private bath, along with a private dressing area.

First floor — 668 sq. ft.
Second floor — 691 sq. ft.
Garage — 2-car

Total living area — 1,359 sq. ft.

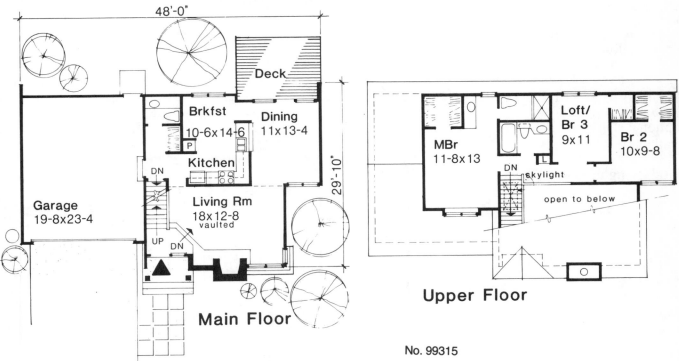

Main Floor

48'-0"

29'-10"

Deck

Brkfst
10-6x14-6

Dining
11x13-4

Kitchen

DN

Garage
19-8x23-4

Living Rm
18x12-8
vaulted

UP   DN

Upper Floor

MBr
11-8x13

Loft/
Br 3
9x11

Br 2
10x9-8

DN

skylight

open to below

No. 99315

Year Round Retreat

No. 90613

This compact home is a bargain to build and designed to save on energy bills. Large glass areas face south, and the dramatic sloping ceiling of the living room allows heat from the wood-burning stove to rise into the upstairs bedrooms through high louvers on the inside wall. In hot weather, just open the windows on both floors for cooling air circulation. Sliding glass doors in the kitchen and living room open to the deck for outdoor dining or relaxation. One bedroom and a full bath complete the first floor. A stair off the foyer ends in a balcony with a commanding view of the living room. Two spacious bedrooms are separated by a full bath.

First floor — 917 sq. ft.
Second floor — 465 sq. ft.
(optional slab construction available)

Total living area — 1,382 sq. ft.

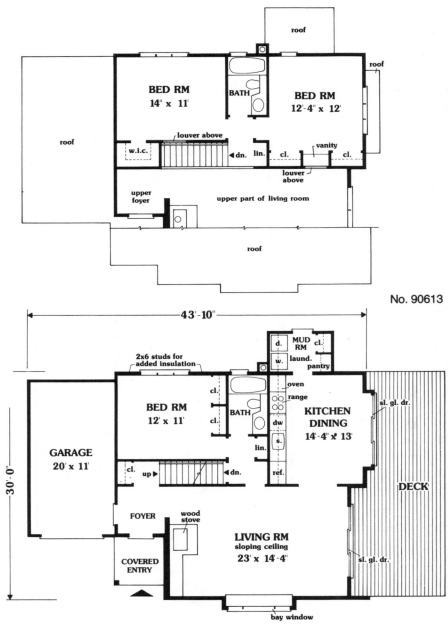

Versatile Chalet

No. 90847

Capture the spirit of the great outdoors
with this versatile chalet designed as
the perfect hide-away for two. The
extra bedroom on the main floor can be
used as a guest bedroom or study, and
all the amenities mean this home could
be used as a compact permanent
residence. The spacious living room
and dining room join the deck through
sliding glass doors.

First floor — 864 sq. ft.
Second floor — 496 sq. ft.
Width — 27'-0"
(plus 5'-0" deck)
Depth — 32'-0"
(plus 8'-0" deck)

Total living area — 1,360 sq. ft.

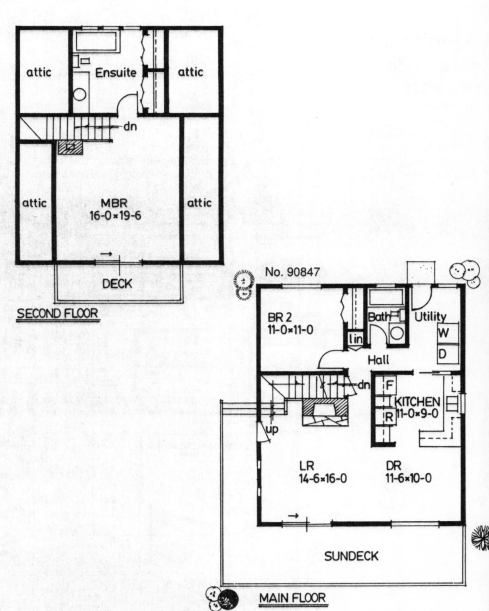

Glass Captures Views & Sun

No. 90121

Abundant glass floods this plan with light and offers images of the surrounding scenery from three sides, as well as serving as a solar energy feature. Large exterior exposed beams crisscross the glass giving a massive, rugged appearance. The center of family activity begins in the family room and proceeds to the deck which flows into a dining patio on the left side. Your family may relax over meals here or in the dining/kitchen area just inside glass doors. Two bedrooms, a full bath and laundry facilities complete the first level. An open wooden stairway beckons you to the second level which opens into a large fireplaced sitting room and balcony overlooking the family room. This plan is available with a basement, crawl space or slab foundation. Please specify when ordering.

First floor — 1,126 sq. ft.
Second floor — 603 sq. ft.

Total living area — 1,729 sq. ft.

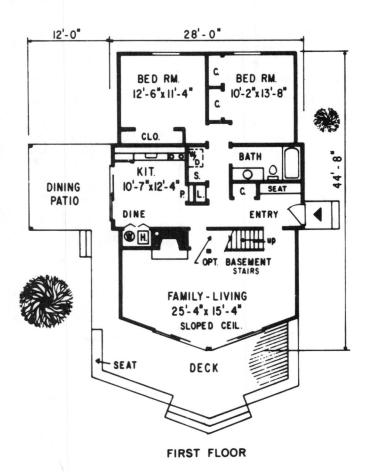

FIRST FLOOR

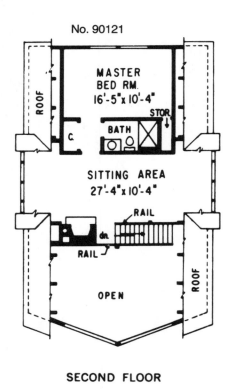

SECOND FLOOR

48

A-Frame for Year-Round Living

No. 90930

If you have a hillside lot, this open design may be just what you've been looking for. With three bedrooms, it's a perfect plan for your growing family. The roomy foyer opens to a hallway that leads to the kitchen, bedrooms, and a dramatic, vaulted living room with a massive fireplace. A wrap-around sundeck gives you lots of outdoor living space. And, upstairs, there's a special retreat — a luxurious master suite complete with its own private deck.

Main floor — 1,238 sq. ft.
Loft — 464 sq. ft.
Basement — 1,175 sq. ft.
Width — 34 ft.
Depth — 56 ft.

Total living area — 1,702 sq. ft.

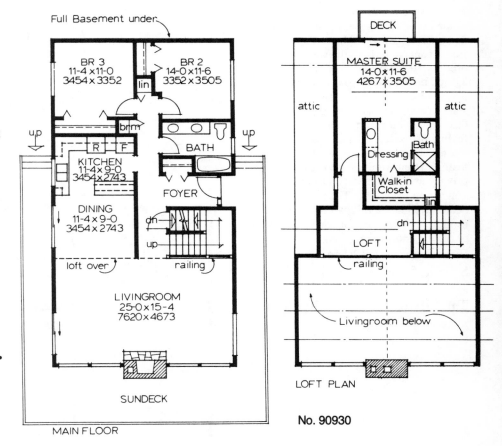

Full Basement under

BR 3
11-4 x 11-0
3454 x 3352

BR 2
14-0 x 11-6
3352 x 3505

lin

BATH

KITCHEN
11-4 x 9-0
3454 x 2743

R F

FOYER

DINING
11-4 x 9-0
3454 x 2743

dn

up

loft over

railing

LIVINGROOM
25-0 x 15-4
7620 x 4673

SUNDECK

MAIN FLOOR

DECK

MASTER SUITE
14-0 x 11-6
4267 x 3505

attic

attic

Dressing

Bath

Walk-in
Closet

lin

dn

LOFT

railing

Livingroom below

LOFT PLAN

No. 90930

Just Add the Sun and Fun

No. 92802

A recipe for vacation bliss. The front of the house sports sliding glass doors and glass windows to the roof, taking full advantage of both the view and the breezes off the water. The wrap-around deck adds to your living space, giving you another place to soak up the sun. Inside, the large dining/living area has a cathedral ceiling, adding to its feeling of space, and a fireplace. The master bedroom has its own private bath. So you won't be giving up your privacy and convenience just because you are on vacation. The secondary bedrooms share a full hall bath. There is a loft area upstairs for added storage or maybe another bedroom.

First floor — 1,320 sq. ft.
Second floor — 185 sq. ft.

Total living area — 1,505 sq. ft.

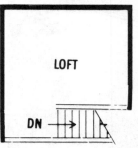

OPEN TO BELOW

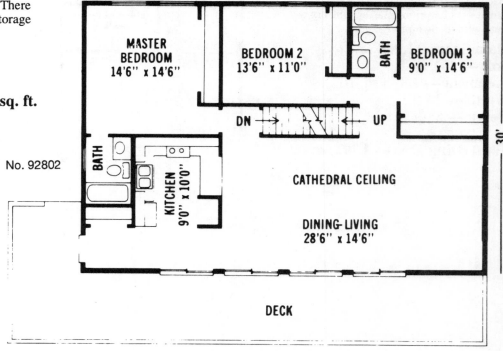

No. 92802

A-Frame Update

No. 90844

Here's a superb home that truly defines the term "open space". You'll feel the spectacular spaciousness of this updated A-frame the moment you walk past the foyer and peek through the galley kitchen. Savor the view through the two-story glass walls in the fireplaced living and dining rooms surrounded by an outdoor deck. Look up at the towering ceilings crowned by an open loft. Even the bedrooms are exceptionally large. The master suite, including a private powder room, and a second bedroom lie at the rear of the first floor adjoining a full bath. The loft overlooking active areas shares the second floor with an expansive bedroom with its own private deck and full bath.

First floor — 1,086 sq. ft.
Second floor — 340 sq. ft.
Total living area — 1,426 sq. ft.

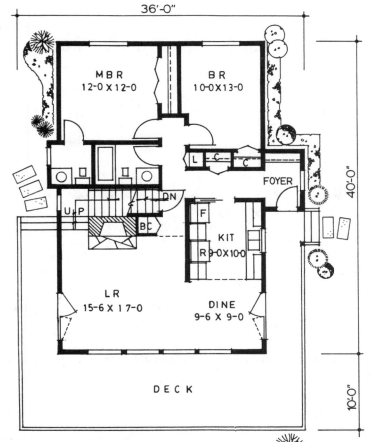

GROUND FLOOR

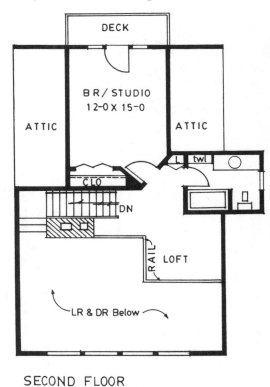

SECOND FLOOR

No. 90844

Old-Fashioned Charm

No. 21124

An old-fashioned, homespun flavor has been created using lattice work, horizontal and vertical placement of wood siding, and full-length front and rear porches with turned wood columns and wood railings. The floor plan features an open living room, dining room and kitchen. A master suite finishes the first level. An additional bedroom and full bath are located upstairs. Here, also, is found a large bonus room which could serve a variety of family needs. Or it can be deleted altogether by adding a second floor balcony overlooking the living room below and allowing the living room ceilings to spaciously rise two full stories. Wood floors throughout the design add a final bit of country to the plan. No materials list available for this plan.

First floor — 835 sq. ft.
Second floor — 817 sq. ft.

Total living area — 1,652 sq. ft.

BONUS ROOM
17⁴ x 23⁰

DRY WASH

BEDROOM 2
10⁸ x 12⁰

ALTERNATE BALCONY
OPEN TO LIVING BELOW

CHASE

BATH 2

45⁴

No. 21124

PORCH

DINING
7⁸ x 8⁰

UP

MASTER
BEDROOM
11⁸ x 12⁰

LIVING
15⁸ x 17⁴

KITCHEN
9⁰ x 10⁰

RANGE

REFRIG.

A/C

HALL

DISHWASHER

DISPL.

M.
BATH

DRESS.

PANTRY

W.H.

PORCH

Skylight Brightens Master Bedroom

No. 34029

Keep dry during the rainy season under the covered porch entry way of this gorgeous home. A foyer separates the dining room with decorative ceiling from the breakfast area and kitchen. Off the kitchen, conveniently located, is the laundry room. The living room features a vaulted beamed ceiling and fireplace. Located between the living room and two bedrooms, both with large closets, is a full bath. On the other side of the living room is the master bedroom. The master bedroom not only has a decorative ceiling, but also a skylight above the entrance of its private bath. The double-vanitied bathroom features a large walk-in closet. For those who enjoy outdoor living, an optional deck is offered, accessible through sliding glass doors off of this wonderful master bedroom. Please indicate slab, crawl space or basement when ordering.

Main living area — 1,698 sq. ft.
Garage — 484 sq. ft.

Total living area — 1,698 sq. ft.

Slab/Crawlspace Option

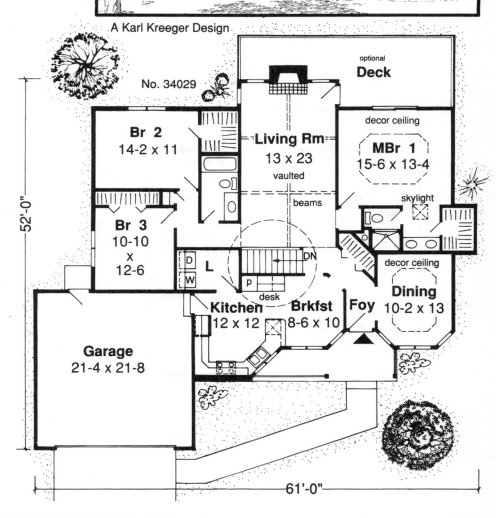

A Karl Kreeger Design

No. 34029

Taking Advantage of the View

No. 92801

Wrap-around decks, sliding glass doors, and lots of windows accent this coastal styled design. The sliding glass doors provide the entrance and the great view on two sides of the home. The efficient kitchen runs in an L-shape to the living room and dining area providing an open, spacious feeling with lots of natural light flowing in. The three bedrooms are to the right of the living/dining area. The master bedroom has its own private bath and the secondary bedrooms share the hall bath. Upstairs, the loft area provides extra living space or perhaps a studio or hobby room.

First floor — 1,296 sq. ft.
Second floor — 144 sq. ft.

Total living area — 1,440 sq. ft.

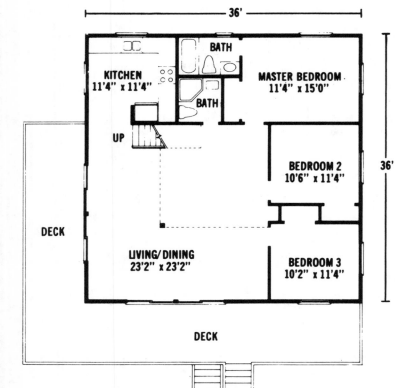

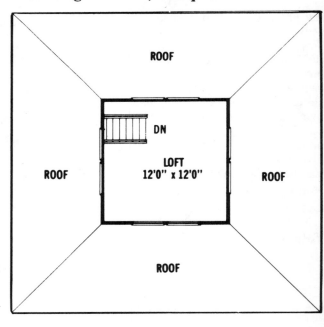

No. 92801

Vacation in Style

No. 92803

This home has a terrific layout for your family's vacation. It has a long wooden deck and a screened in porch allowing for added living space. The Great room/dining area is large and has a fireplace to warm up those cool evenings. The efficient kitchen has ample work and cabinet space. All the bedrooms are located at the right side of the home. The master bedroom has a walk-in closet. There are two full baths allowing easy access from all the bedrooms. A laundry room is located at the rear of the house so that vacation time is not wasted going out to do laundry. Enough living space to insure everyone an enjoyable vacation.

Main living area — 1,600 sq. ft.

— 48' —

Total living area — 1,600 sq. ft.

BEDROOM 4
11'0" x 9'6"

MASTER BEDROOM
13'6" x 13'4"

SCREENED PORCH
8'0" x 24'0"

GREAT ROOM/ DINING
19'6" x 23'0"

KITCHEN
11'6" x 12'0"

BATH

WIC

BATH

LAUNDRY

40'

DECK
14'0" x 4'0"

BEDROOM 3
11'0" x 9'6"

BEDROOM 2
11'0" x 9'6"

No. 92803

Compact and Efficient

No. 10751

Building this cozy cottage won't break the bank. Slab construction, elimination of extra hallway space, and stacked plumbing will keep your budget under control. But, efficiency doesn't mean you have to sacrifice beauty. The spacious, fireplaced living room seems even larger with its soaring ceilings. A galley kitchen, full bath, and roomy bedroom complete the first floor. View the scene below from the balcony, which leads to a second bedroom, full bath, and a sewing room that could double as a home office or den.

First floor — 660 sq. ft.
Second floor — 330 sq. ft.

Total living area — 990 sq. ft.

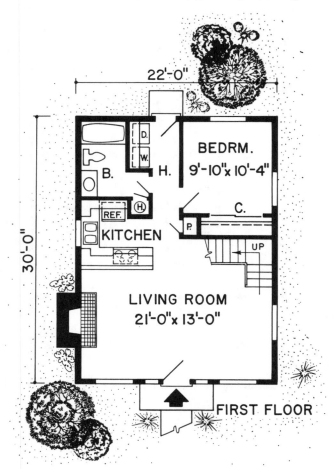

FIRST FLOOR

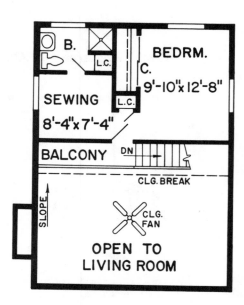

SECOND FLOOR

No. 10751

All Seasons

No. 91319

From the foyer of this home an open stairway leads to the upstairs study and the master bedroom, which has a private bath and walk-in wardrobe. The kitchen with breakfast bar opens into the dining area, which in turn merges with the vaulted-ceiling, stone fireplaced living room. The full, daylight basement features a variety of rooms to serve storage, laundry, and mudroom purposes with an adjacent full bath. A non-basement version of this plan is also available.

Main floor — 1,306 sq. ft.
Upper floor — 598 sq. ft.
Lower floor — 1,288 sq ft.

Total living area — 3,192 sq. ft.

MAIN FLR.

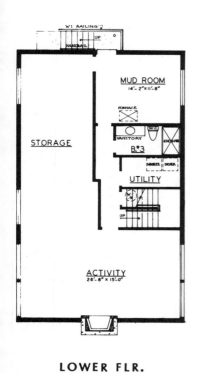

LOWER FLR.

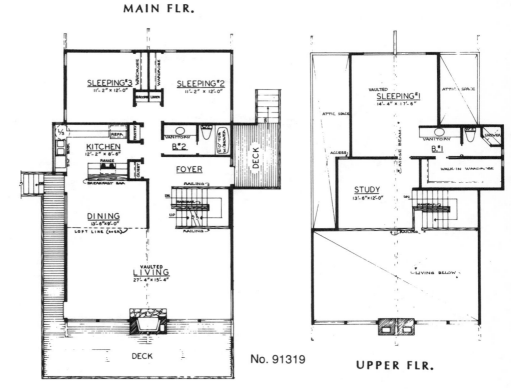

No. 91319

UPPER FLR.

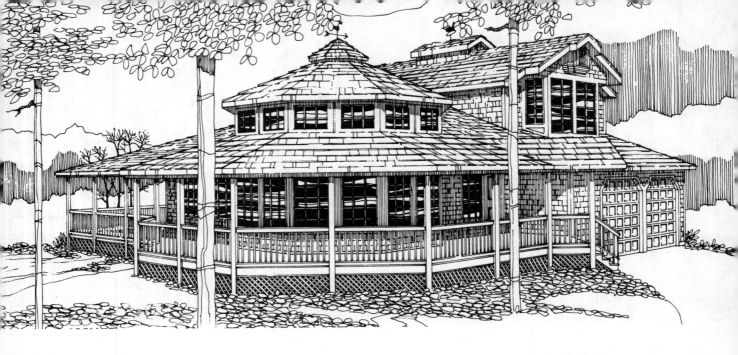

Deck Surrounds House on Three Sides

No. 91304

Sitting in the sunken, circular living room of this elegant family home, you'll feel like you're outdoors even when you're not. Windows on four sides combine with a vaulted clerestory for a wide-open feeling you'll love year-round. When it's warm, throw open the windows, or relax on the deck. But, when there's a chill in the air, back-to-back fireplaces keep the atmosphere toasty in the living room and adjoining Great room. Even the convenient kitchen, with its bay dining nook, enjoys a backyard view. Do you sew? You'll love this roomy spot just steps away from the kitchen. Bump-out and bay windows give the three upstairs bedrooms a cheerful atmosphere and cozy sitting nooks.

First floor — 1,372 sq. ft.
Second floor — 858 sq. ft.

Total living area — 2,230 sq. ft.

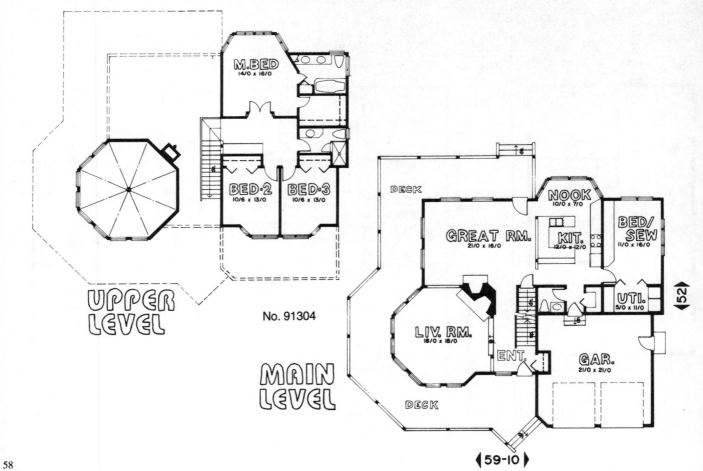

No. 91304

Master Suite on a Private Level

No. 26810

With its four floors staggered at half-level intervals, this house is both architecturally fascinating and effectively planned. Entering on the third level, one sees dining and sunken living rooms ahead on a space-expanded diagonal. The corridor kitchen extends into a traffic-free space open to living areas on one side. A deck makes the outdoors a natural part of all social areas. One half-level higher, the master bedroom connects to a study, a deck and a luxurious compartmental bathroom. On the second level, two smaller bedrooms have a landing with a bath and a convenient laundry. The lowest level of the house is a recreation basement. The framing of this house uses large studs and rafters spaced at wide intervals to cut construction time, reduce the need for lumber, and open deeper gaps for thicker insulating batts.

Upper level — 1,423 sq. ft.
Lower level — 1,420 sq. ft.
Garage — 478 sq. ft.

Total living area — 2,843 sq. ft.

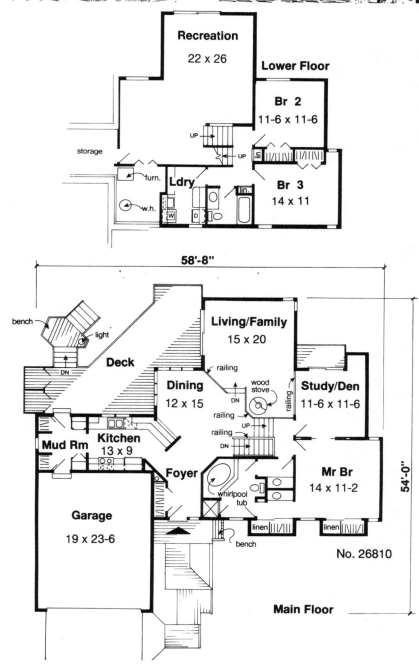

Coved Ceilings
Accent Design

No. 91644

A striking roofline and aristocratic profile serve notice to all that the days of fine living have not passed. The interior is designed with todays busy professional in mind. Compactness with no sacrifice of luxury. Coved ceilings, ample closet space and wrap-around kitchen. With a cozy fireplace in the living room it's just what the doctor ordered after a busy day at the office.

Main living area — 1,687 sq. ft.

Total living area — 1,687 sq. ft.

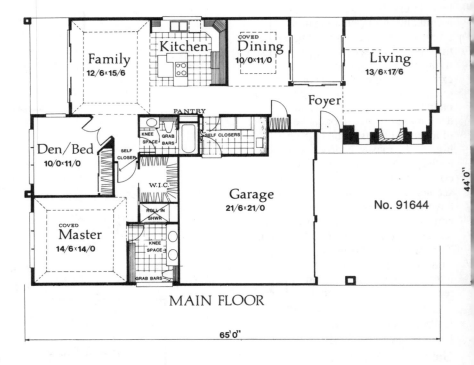

No. 91644

MAIN FLOOR

65'0"

44'0"

Family 12/6×15/6
Kitchen
Dining 10/0×11/0
Living 13/6×17/6
Foyer
Den/Bed 10/0×11/0
Master 14/6×14/0 COVED
Garage 21/6×21/0
PANTRY
KNEE SPACE
GRAB BARS
SELF CLOSERS
SELF CLOSER
W.I.C.
ROLL IN SHWR
KNEE SPACE
GRAB BARS

Accessibility Features
➤ Level entry way
➤ Ramp with entry level landing
➤ Wide doorways (32"-36" clear width)
➤ Low-pile carpeting with thin padding
➤ Chair-height electrical controls/outlets
➤ Direct outside emergency exit from bedroom in some cases
➤ Reinforced walls (i.e. 3/4" plywood backing throughout) for installation of grab bars

Open Spaces Aid Accessibility

No. 91653

Dramatically steep rooflines and a large arched picture window create a stunning front to this simplistic yet stylish home. Once inside, you're immediately drawn to the living room; impressive with its coved ceiling, large windows and fireplace. The home's easy-flowing floor plan beckons you to move from room-to-room. The expansive L-shaped kitchen with cooking island and wetbar leads you to the den and coved family room with its view through large picture windows, or to the coved master bedroom to relax. Every room in this special home is easily accessible, and the entire home is barrier-free. It's a lifetime home and was specially designed to be fully adaptable for anyone with a disability.

Main living area — 1,889 sq. ft.

Garage — 2-car

Total living area — 1,889 sq. ft.

Accessibility Features

➤ Level entry way
➤ Ramp with entry level landing
➤ Wide doorways (32"-36" clear width)
➤ Low-pile carpeting with thin padding
➤ Chair-height electrical controls/outlets
➤ Direct outside emergency exit from bedroom in some cases
➤ Reinforced walls (i.e. 3/4" plywood backing throughout) for installation of grab bars

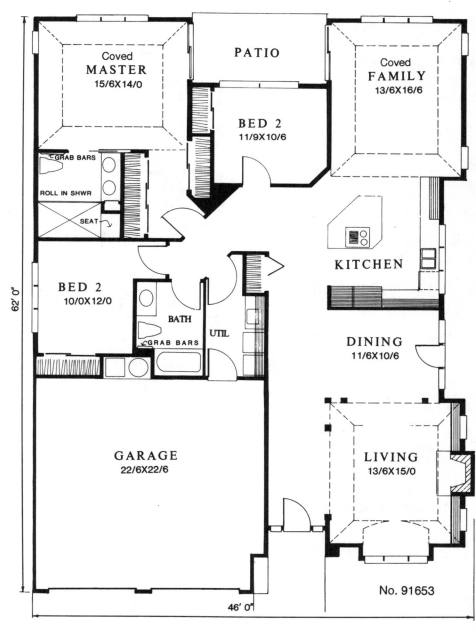

Coved MASTER 15/6X14/0

PATIO

Coved FAMILY 13/6X16/6

GRAB BARS

ROLL IN SHWR

SEAT

BED 2 11/9X10/6

KITCHEN

BED 2 10/0X12/0

BATH

GRAB BARS

UTIL

DINING 11/6X10/6

GARAGE 22/6X22/6

LIVING 13/6X15/0

62' 0"

46' 0"

No. 91653

A Ranch with Aesthetic Qualities

No. 91683

This deceptively simple dwelling boasts many features normally found only in much larger homes. This popular plan has been redesigned to allow accessiblity for a lifetime of use. Wider hallways and doors, specially designed baths and kitchens are among some of the features you will find. This plan gives you aesthetic qualities as well as practicality.

Main living area — 1,418 sq. ft.
Garage — 390 sq. ft.

Total living area — 1,418 sq. ft.

Accessibility Features

➤ Level entry way
➤ Ramp with entry level landing
➤ Wide doorways (32"-36" clear width)
➤ Low-pile carpeting with thin padding
➤ Chair-height electrical controls/outlets
➤ Direct outside emergency exit from bedroom in some cases
➤ Reinforced walls (i.e. 3/4" plywood backing throughout) for installation of grab bars

ROLL IN SHWR
GRAB BARS
Master 14/0X12/6
Living 12/6X15/6
Dining 10/0X11/6
GRAB BARS
BATH
Nook 9/6X9/0
Entry
COVED
Bedrm. 2 10/6X10/0
Bedrm. 3 10/0X10/0
UTIL
PANTRY
Kitchen
50'0"

MAIN FLOOR
No. 91683

Garage 20/0x19/6

50'0"

Functional Home With Distinct Features

No. 91646

This deceptively simple plan describes a functional home with features usually found only in much larger dwellings. Although at 50'x50', it will fit on almost any lot. There are three bedrooms and a den. The master bedroom with double doors, his-n-her sinks and a spacious walk-in closet give a taste of luxury. The modern kitchen enjoys easy access to all parts of the home and boasts a utility room of generous size.

Main living area — 1,422 sq. ft.

Total living area — 1,422 sq. ft.

Accessibility Features

➤ Level entry way
➤ Ramp with entry level landing
➤ Wide doorways (32"-36" clear width)
➤ Low-pile carpeting with thin padding
➤ Chair-height electrical controls/outlets
➤ Direct outside emergency exit from bedroom in some cases
➤ Reinforced walls (i.e. 3/4" plywood backing throughout) for installation of grab bars

MASTER 14/0X12/0
LIVING 12/6X14/0
DINING 11/0X10/0
ROLL IN SHWR
GRAB BARS
KITCHEN
BED 2 10/6X10/0
BED 3 10/0X10/0
ENTRY
DEN 12/0X10/0
UTIL
SELF CLOSER
GARAGE 20/0X19/6
MAIN FLOOR
No. 91646
50'0"
50'0"

Hillside Haven

No. 91623

Do you have a hillside lot that slopes down from the road? With its ground floor family room and bedrooms overlooking the rear patio, this handsome home reserves its upper floor for spacious active areas and a spectacular view of the surrounding yard. The expansive entry foyer opens to a gracious, fireplaced living room with coved ceilings that are mirrored in the adjoining dining room. Step straight back to the island kitchen, which features a sink peninsula facing the huge windows in the adjoining nook. Access the rear deck here, or from the coved master suite behind the garage. You'll relish the privacy of your own, compartmentalized bath,

walk-in closet, and deckside view.

Main floor — 1,418 sq. ft.
Lower floor — 1,054 sq. ft.
Garage — 2-car

Total living area — 2,472 sq. ft.

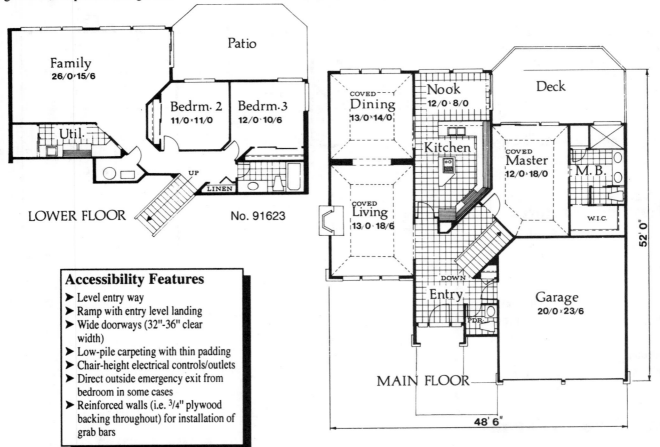

Accessibility Features

➤ Level entry way
➤ Ramp with entry level landing
➤ Wide doorways (32"-36" clear width)
➤ Low-pile carpeting with thin padding
➤ Chair-height electrical controls/outlets
➤ Direct outside emergency exit from bedroom in some cases
➤ Reinforced walls (i.e. 3/4" plywood backing throughout) for installation of grab bars

Carefree and Cozy

No. 91618

The multiple peaks of this one-level home hint at the intriguing plan you'll find inside. The central foyer opens to a many-sided great hall, which offers access to every area of the house. To the left, the fireplaced living room with coved ceilings and massive front window flows into a formal dining room with built-in corner cabinet. Step back to the island kitchen that adjoins a sunny breakfast bay and comfortable family room overlooking the deck. You'll find three bedrooms tucked behind the garage, off a hallway that leads past the den, powder room, full bath, and utility room with garage access. The master suite at the rear of the house is a special treat, with its bay window, coved ceilings, and private bath with double vanities and garden spa.

Main living area — 2,087 sq. ft.
Garage — 2-car

Total living area — 2,087 sq. ft.

Accessibility Features

➤ Level entry way
➤ Ramp with entry level landing
➤ Wide doorways (32"-36" clear width)
➤ Low-pile carpeting with thin padding
➤ Chair-height electrical controls/outlets
➤ Direct outside emergency exit from bedroom in some cases
➤ Reinforced walls (i.e. 3/4" plywood backing throughout) for installation of grab bars

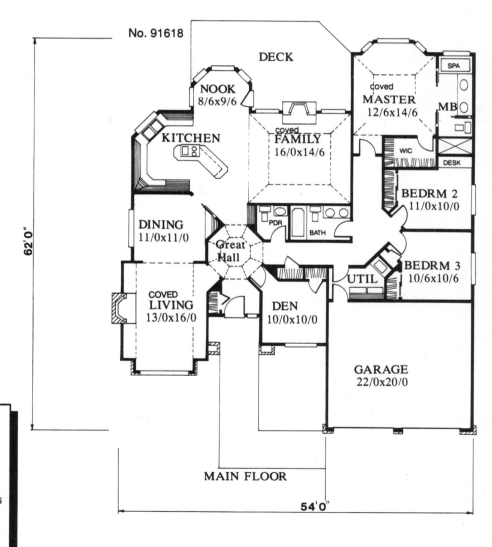

No. 91618

DECK

NOOK 8/6x9/6

KITCHEN

coved FAMILY 16/0x14/6

coved MASTER 12/6x14/6

SPA

MB

WIC

DESK

BEDRM 2 11/0x10/0

DINING 11/0x11/0

PDR

BATH

Great Hall

BEDRM 3 10/6x10/6

UTIL

COVED LIVING 13/0x16/0

DEN 10/0x10/0

GARAGE 22/0x20/0

62'0"

MAIN FLOOR

54'0"

Classic Compact Home

No. 91642

For the busy professionl couple. Compact style is the word here, and the brick and classic lines suggest a country cottage. Within are all the comforts of home, coved master bedroom, wetbar, fireplace, modern kitchen with a central island. And, best of all, only 1,307 square feet to clean!

Main living area — 1,307 sq. ft.

Accessibility Features

➤ Level entry way
➤ Ramp with entry level landing
➤ Wide doorways (32"-36" clear width)
➤ Low-pile carpeting with thin padding
➤ Chair-height electrical controls/outlets
➤ Direct outside emergency exit from bedroom in some cases
➤ Reinforced walls (i.e. 3/4" plywood backing throughout) for installation of grab bars

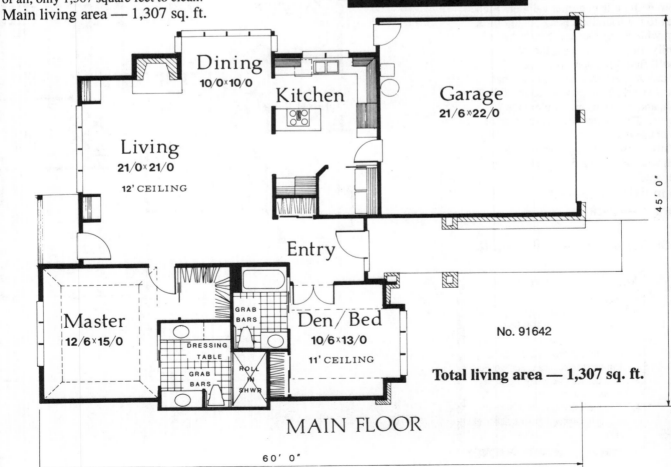

Dining
10/0 × 10/0

Kitchen

Garage
21/6 × 22/0

Living
21/0 × 21/0

12' CEILING

Entry

Master
12/6 × 15/0

GRAB BARS

DRESSING TABLE

GRAB BARS

ROLL IN SHWR

Den/Bed
10/6 × 13/0

11' CEILING

No. 91642

Total living area — 1,307 sq. ft.

MAIN FLOOR

45' 0"

60' 0"

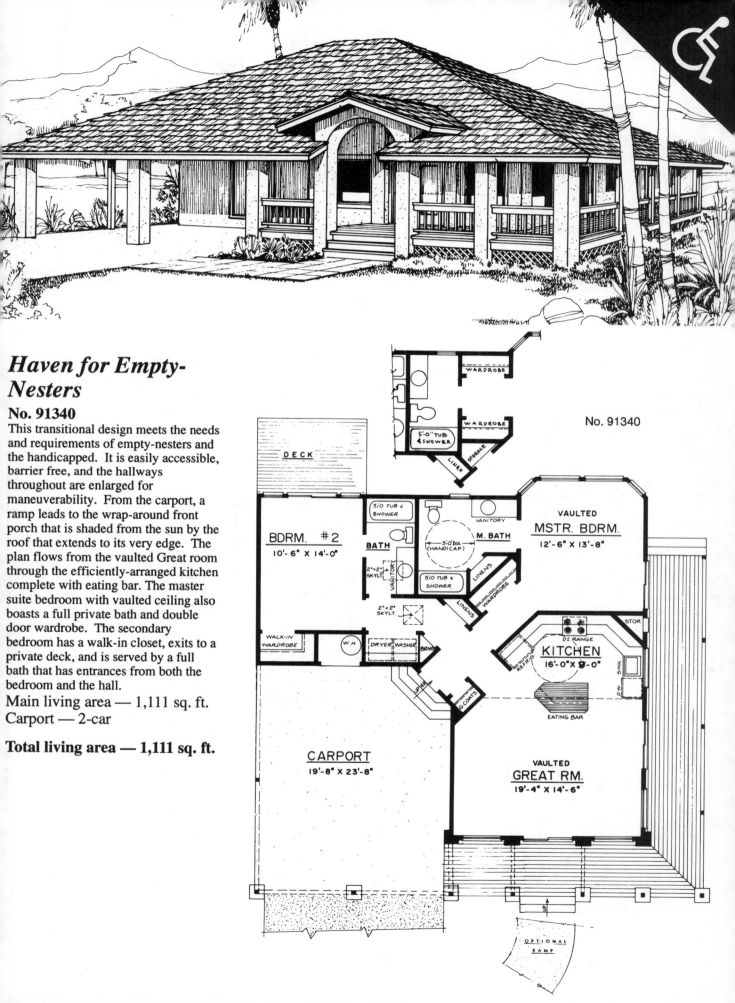

Haven for Empty-Nesters

No. 91340

This transitional design meets the needs and requirements of empty-nesters and the handicapped. It is easily accessible, barrier free, and the hallways throughout are enlarged for maneuverability. From the carport, a ramp leads to the wrap-around front porch that is shaded from the sun by the roof that extends to its very edge. The plan flows from the vaulted Great room through the efficiently-arranged kitchen complete with eating bar. The master suite bedroom with vaulted ceiling also boasts a full private bath and double door wardrobe. The secondary bedroom has a walk-in closet, exits to a private deck, and is served by a full bath that has entrances from both the bedroom and the hall.

Main living area — 1,111 sq. ft.
Carport — 2-car

Total living area — 1,111 sq. ft.

No. 91340

DECK

WARDROBE

WARDROBE

5'-0" TUB & SHOWER

LINEN

STORAGE

BDRM. #2
10'-6" X 14'-0"

5/0 TUB & SHOWER

BATH

VANITORY

5'-0" DIA (HANDICAP)

M. BATH

VAULTED
MSTR. BDRM.
12'-6" X 13'-8"

2'x2' SKYLT

VANITORY

5/0 TUB & SHOWER

LINENS

WARDROBE

2'x2' SKYLT

LINENS

WALK-IN WARDROBE

W. H.

DRYER WASHER

BRM.

UP RR

COATS

STOR.

DI RANGE

REFRIG

KITCHEN
16'-0" X 9'-0"

D.W.

SINK

EATING BAR

CARPORT
19'-8" X 23'-8"

VAULTED
GREAT RM.
19'-4" X 14'-6"

OPTIONAL RAMP

Yours for a Lifetime

No. 91651

A home of distinction...from the large bay windows in the living room, to the vaulted ceilings and expansive foyer and kitchen, this two-plus bedroom, two bath home is truly unique and stunning. Especially charming is the breakfast nook where you can casually enjoy a meal in front of the double doors that overlook the porch. The plan is designed as a lifetime home and includes such attractive amenities as a roll-in shower, wide hallways for easier wheelchair mobility, and lower workspaces that are accessible to anyone with a disability.

Main living area — 1,653 sq. ft.
Garage — 2-car

Total living area — 1,653 sq. ft.

Accessibility Features

➤ Level entry way
➤ Ramp with entry level landing
➤ Wide doorways (32"-36" clear width)
➤ Low-pile carpeting with thin padding
➤ Chair-height electrical controls/outlets
➤ Direct outside emergency exit from bedroom in some cases
➤ Reinforced walls (i.e. 3/4" plywood backing throughout) for installation of grab bars

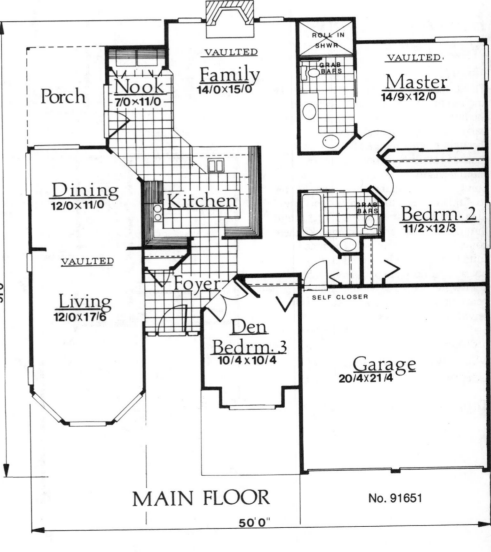

Porch

Nook
7/0 × 11/0

VAULTED
Family
14/0 × 15/0

ROLL IN
SHWR
GRAB
BARS

VAULTED
Master
14/9 × 12/0

Dining
12/0 × 11/0

Kitchen

GRAB
BARS

Bedrm. 2
11/2 × 12/3

VAULTED

Foyer

SELF CLOSER

Living
12/0 × 17/6

Den
Bedrm. 3
10/4 × 10/4

Garage
20/4 × 21/4

51'0"

MAIN FLOOR   No. 91651

50'0"

With Accessibility In Mind

No. 91684

This contemporary home has a hint of the traditional. The first floor includes a large formal living room with a coved ceiling to add interest. The living room flows right into the formal dining room for easy entertaining. The kitchen has an efficient layout and includes a pantry. Conveniently located off the kitchen is the family room and for informal dining, the eating nook. The master suite also has a coved ceiling and features a master bath with a double vanity and roll in shower. Upstairs, designed with a stair lift in mind, you will find three more nice-sized bedrooms, two baths, an alcove and bonus space. Yes, this home was designed for accessibility throughout.

Main floor — 1,632 sq. ft.
Second floor — 776 sq. ft.
Bonus — 312 sq. ft.

Total living area — 2,720 sq. ft.

Accessibility Features
➤ Level entry way
➤ Ramp with entry level landing
➤ Wide doorways (32"-36" clear width)
➤ Low-pile carpeting with thin padding
➤ Chair-height electrical controls/outlets
➤ Direct outside emergency exit from bedroom in some cases
➤ Reinforced walls (i.e. 3/4" plywood backing throughout) for installation of grab bars

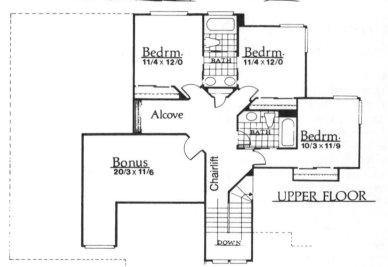

Bedrm. 11/4 x 12/0
BATH
Bedrm. 11/4 x 12/0
Alcove
BATH
Bedrm. 10/3 x 11/9
Bonus 20/3 x 11/6
Chairlift
DOWN
UPPER FLOOR

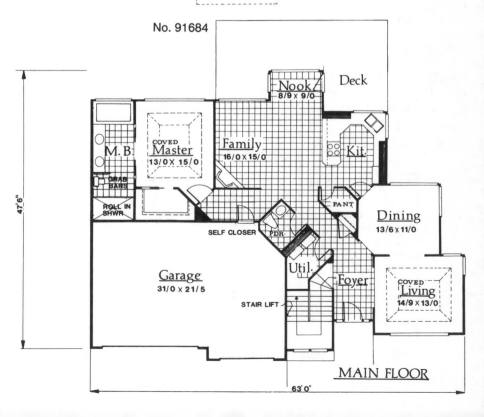

No. 91684

Nook 8/9 x 9/0
Deck
COVED Master 13/0 X 15/0
Family 16/0 x 15/0
Kit.
M. B.
GRAB BARS
ROLL IN SHWR
SELF CLOSER
PDR.
PANT
Dining 13/6 x 11/0
Garage 31/0 x 21/5
Util.
Foyer
COVED Living 14/9 x 13/0
STAIR LIFT
47'6"
63'0"
MAIN FLOOR

Home Grows To Suit Your Needs

No. 91628

This compact charmer offers spacious active areas, four bedrooms, and plenty of growing room. The towering foyer is tucked between the garage and the sunny living room with its partially vaulted ceiling. Step back past the open staircase to reach the island kitchen, which serves both the formal dining room and sunny informal nook with equal efficiency. The cozy family room, with its huge fireplace and sliders to the rear deck, is a special gathering place in any weather. Upstairs, you'll find three bedrooms served by a double-vanitied hall bath, and a master suite that boasts a private bath with both spa and step-in shower. Finish the bonus room over the garage now, or wait until later.

First floor — 1,085 sq. ft.
Second floor — 941 sq. ft.
Bonus — 238 sq. ft.
Garage — 3-car

Total living area — 2,264 sq. ft.

No. 91628

UPPER FLOOR

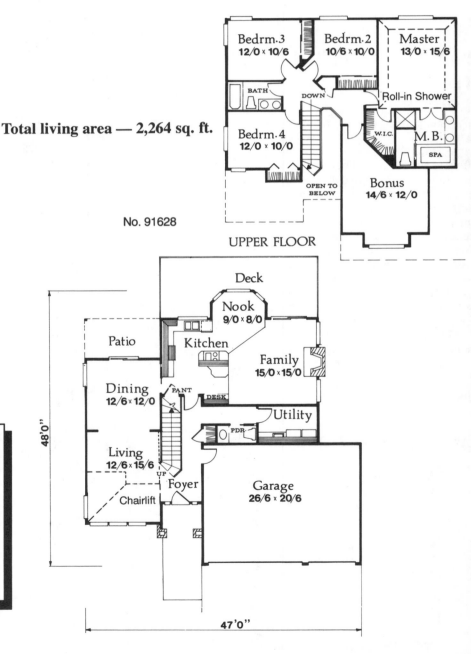

Accessibility Features

➤ Level entry way
➤ Ramp with entry level landing
➤ Wide doorways (32"-36" clear width)
➤ Low-pile carpeting with thin padding
➤ Chair-height electrical controls/outlets
➤ Direct outside emergency exit from bedroom in some cases
➤ Reinforced walls (i.e. 3/4" plywood backing throughout) for installation of grab bars

Ideal Family Plan

No. 91647

Ideal for the family with a small child. The second bedroom is adjacent to the master bedroom, so that mom and dad can rest easily knowing that their precious one is within earshot. The den is large enough to double as a bedroom when company calls. There are separate living, dining and family rooms, the later complete with wet bar. All this in 1,444 square feet.

Main living area — 1,444 sq. ft.

Total living area — 1,444 sq. ft.

Accessibility Features

➤ Level entry way
➤ Ramp with entry level landing
➤ Wide doorways (32"-36" clear width)
➤ Low-pile carpeting with thin padding
➤ Chair-height electrical controls/outlets
➤ Direct outside emergency exit from bedroom in some cases
➤ Reinforced walls (i.e. ³/₄" plywood backing throughout) for installation of grab bars

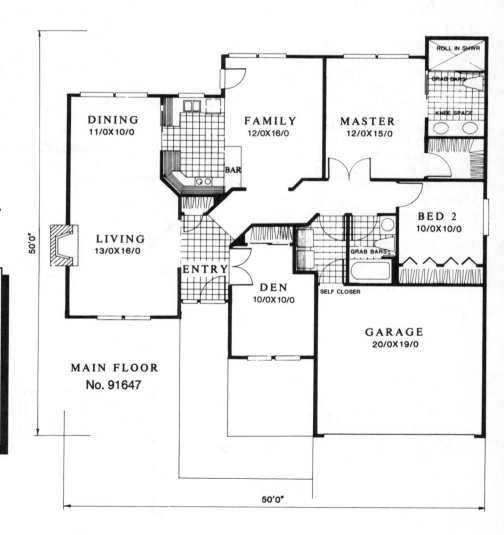

MAIN FLOOR
No. 91647

A Lifetime Home

No. 91662

This beautiful, very popular plan has been re-designed to allow accessibility for a lifetime of use. It has built-in features that make modification possible to accommodate the permanently disabled, the elderly or even temporary disabled due to sports injuries, surgery, etc... Wider hallways and doors, specially designed baths and kitchen, and low profile thresholds are among some of the features you will find.

Main floor — 2,167 sq. ft.
Lower Floor — 1,154 sq. ft.

Total living area — 3,321 sq. ft.

Accessibility Features

➤ Level entry way
➤ Ramp with entry level landing
➤ Wide doorways (32"-36" clear width)
➤ Low-pile carpeting with thin padding
➤ Chair-height electrical controls/outlets
➤ Direct outside emergency exit from bedroom in some cases
➤ Reinforced walls (i.e. 3/4" plywood backing throughout) for installation of grab bars

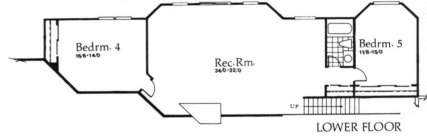

LOWER FLOOR

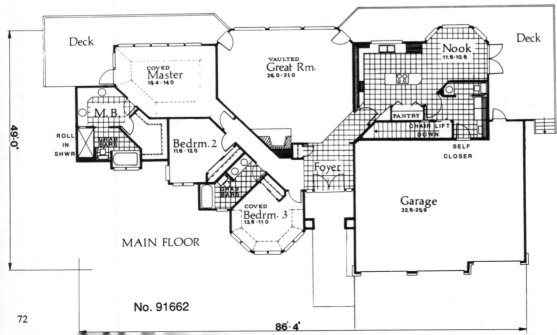

MAIN FLOOR

No. 91662

Adaptable For the Disabled

No. 91652

The charming and cozy exterior of this two-plus bedroom, two bath home does not prepare you for the drama within. Elegant arched doorways lead you to the living and family rooms. Entertain in the dining room, warm up to a cozy fireplace or study in the den; comfort abounds in every room of this warm home. Designed as a lifetime home, it is handicap accessible and has convenient, luxurious features such as an expansive kitchen with walk-in pantry and breakfast nook, and a large walk-in closet in the master bedroom.

Main living area — 1,541 sq. ft.

Garage — 2-car

Total living area — 1,541 sq. ft.

Accessibility Features

➤ Level entry way
➤ Ramp with entry level landing
➤ Wide doorways (32"-36" clear width)
➤ Low-pile carpeting with thin padding
➤ Chair-height electrical controls/outlets
➤ Direct outside emergency exit from bedroom in some cases
➤ Reinforced walls (i.e. 3/4" plywood backing throughout) for installation of grab bars

No. 91652

Dining
11/0X10/0

Family
12/0X17/0

Master
12/0X14/0

ROLL IN SHWR

GRAB BARS

KNEE SPACE

Living
13/0X16/0

ARCH

GRAB BARS

Bedrm. 2
10/0X10/0

Entry

Bedrm. 3/Den
11/0X10/0

Garage
20/0X19/0

MAIN FLOOR

50'0"

50'0"

Compact and Convenient

No. 91341

Ideal for either a vacation or retirement home, this house is also designed to be handicap accessible. From the covered front porch, the spacious foyer leads to both the bedroom wing and the large open family living areas. The living room, dining room, and kitchen all share one large area in such a way that no one need be excluded from conversation or activities. Angles in the kitchen add interest and allow for an abundance of cabinets and counter work space. An island is also featured with a sink and breakfast bar. The living room has access to a covered rear deck, with skylight, through a sliding glass door. The dining room accesses a second covered rear deck, and also has two large windows to help brighten the area, as well as the kitchen. The bedroom wing features the master bedroom suite with access through a French door to the covered rear deck, and a personal bath which is handicap accessible. A den/bedroom with a second full bath complete the bedroom wing.

Main living area — 1,170 sq. ft.

Total living area — 1,170 sq. ft.

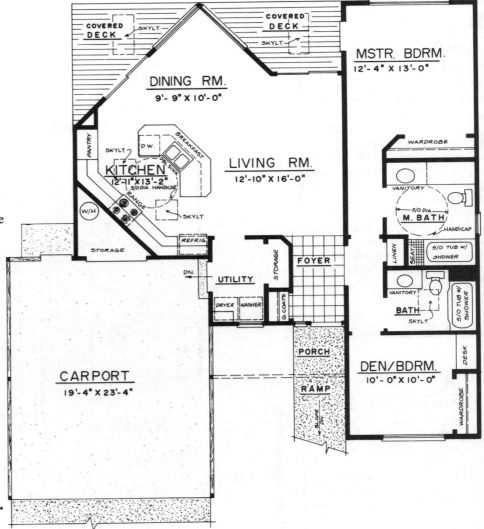

No. 91341

Dramatic Shape and Features

No. 10274

If your lot is the right shape, build this magnificent plan. A dramatically positioned fireplace forms the focus of a contemporary living area. Kitchen, dining, and living spaces are fashioned into a huge central room that flows from the heart of the home through sliding doors to the dramatic deck. The many flexible decorating options, such as screens and room dividers or conversational groupings, are impressive. A huge master bedroom and two roomy bedrooms are tucked in a wing away from the main area for privacy.

Main living area — 1,783 sq. ft.
Garage — 576 sq. ft.

Total living area — 1,783 sq. ft.

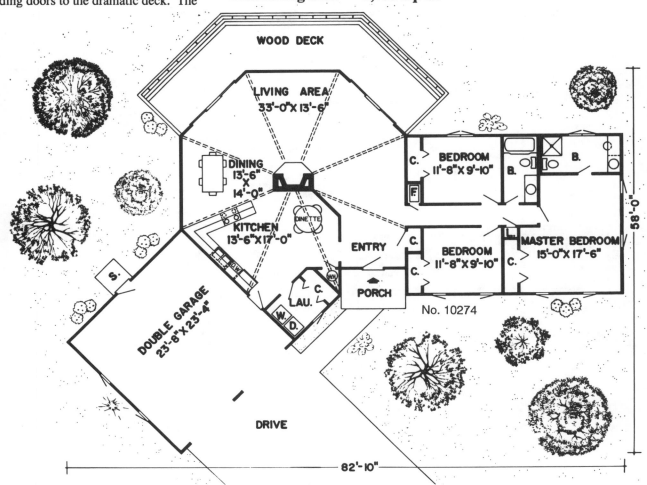

Trim Plan Designed for Handicapped

No. 10360

Attractive and accessible, this three bedroom home has been carefully detailed to provide both comfort and self-sufficiency for the handicapped individual. Ramps allow entry to garage, patio and porch. Doors and windows are located so that they can be opened with ease, and both baths feature wall-hung toilets at a special 16'-18" height. Spacious rooms, wide halls, and the oversized double garage allow a wheelchair to be maneuvered with minimal effort, and the sink and cooktop are also located with this in mind.

Main living area — 1,882 sq. ft.
Garage — 728 sq. ft.

Total living area — 1,882 sq. ft.

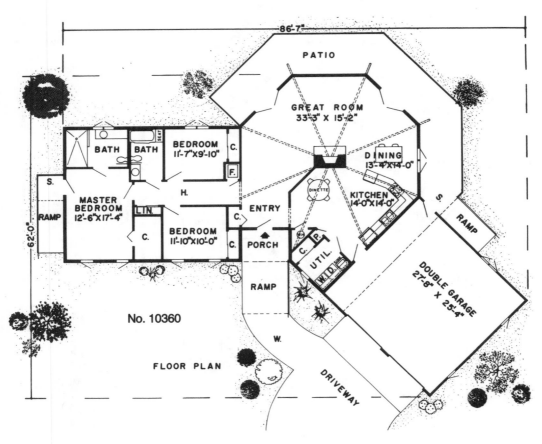

No. 10360

FLOOR PLAN

Ranch with Handicapped Access

No. 20403

This comfortable Ranch has the convenience of an open floor plan as well as handicapped access from the front door, garage and deck. Life centers in the area surrounding the galley kitchen. The family room has a large hearth and fireplace, and opens onto an extensive deck off the rear of the house. The space-saving kitchen serves both a formal dining room and a sunny, bow-windowed breakfast room. Cathedral ceilings in the master bedroom set off a wall of windows. A walk-in closet and a bath designed for handicapped use are also included. The other two bedrooms share a full bath. This plan is built on a crawl space foundation.

Main living area — 1,734 sq. ft.
Porch — 118 sq. ft.
Deck — 354 sq. ft.
Garage — 606 sq. ft.

Total living area — 1,734 sq. ft.

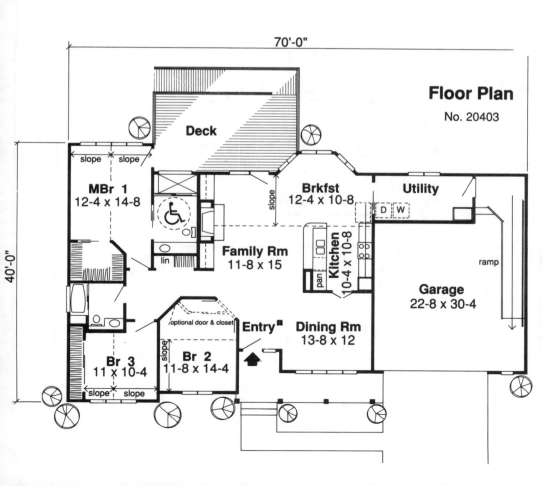

Floor Plan

No. 20403

70'-0"

40'-0"

Deck

MBr 1
12-4 x 14-8

slope   slope

lin

Family Rm
11-8 x 15

slope

Brkfst
12-4 x 10-8

Utility

D   W

Kitchen
10-4 x 10-8

pan

Garage
22-8 x 30-4

ramp

optional door & closet

slope

Entry

Br 3
11 x 10-4

Br 2
11-8 x 14-4

slope   slope

Dining Rm
13-8 x 12

Carefree Convenience

No. 20402

Although this adaptable, one-level gem features handicap accessibility, it's an excellent choice for anyone looking for an easy-care home. Notice the extra-wide hallways, the master bath with roll-in shower, and specially designed kitchen with roll-out pantry and counters designed for wheelchair access. A sunny, spacious atmosphere envelopes each room, thanks to generous windows and sloping ceilings. Reach the deck from the U-shaped kitchen overlooking the fireplaced family room, and from the master suite. The dining room and living room, separated by a handy bar and just steps away from the kitchen, are ideal for entertaining. A hall bath serves the front bedrooms.

Main living area — 2,153 sq. ft.
Garage — 617 sq. ft.
Porch — 210 sq. ft.

Total living area — 2,153 sq. ft.

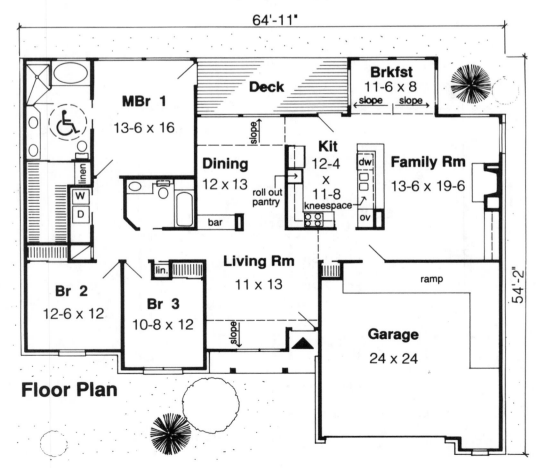

Floor Plan

Design Highlighted By Split Roofline

No. 90028

Modern and up-to-date is the best way to describe this design which is highlighted by the vertical siding and dramatic split roofline. To make this energy-efficient home, the steeply raked roof should face south, to obtain maximum solar benefits for the flat-plate collector panels. Other energy saving devices are: solar domestic hot water system, double glazed windows and sliding doors, 6" thick insulation in the wall, 9" thick insulation in ceilings and weatherstripping. The living-dining area features a massive stone-faced heat circulating fireplace that radiates warmth to the interior of the house.

First floor — 960 sq. ft.
Second floor — 580 sq. ft.
Wood deck — 460 sq. ft.

Total living area — 1,540 sq. ft.

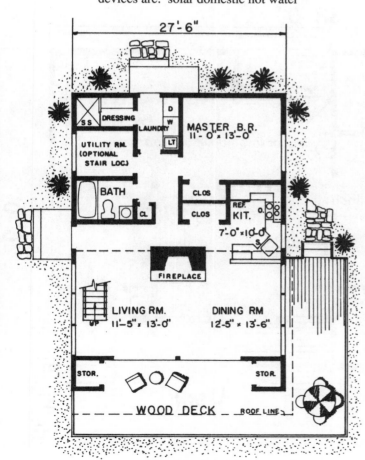

FIRST FLOOR

No. 90028

SECOND FLOOR

Relaxing Retreat

No. 24309

Take a vacation from the everyday stresses you endure in a home that takes your cares away. All the living area of this home is on one floor. The fireplaced living room is a nice size and flows easily into the dining and kitchen areas. These open areas create a feeling spaciousness. The wrap-around deck in the front of the home has a built in bar-b-que for easy outdoor cooking. The glass, double door entry with floor-to-ceiling glass on either side lets you enjoy the outdoors from inside while allowing lots of natural light to flow in. The bedrooms are a nice size and have ample closet space. Storage space could also include the loft area. This home could easily be turned into a retirement residence.

Main living area — 792 sq. ft.

Total living area — 792 sq. ft.

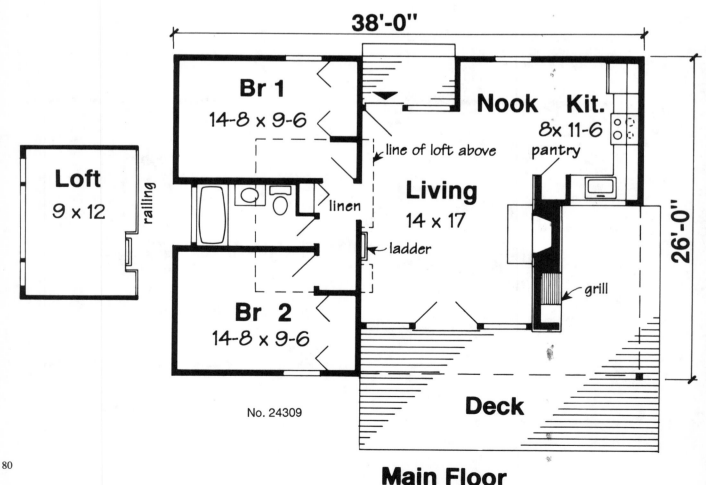

Stacked Windows Brighten Modern Design

No. 90813

A massive fireplace dominates the soaring, spacious living/dining room of this sunny, compact home with wrap-around deck. A convenient rear entry leads from utility room to breakfast nook and kitchen. The master bedroom and a full bath complete the first floor. Clerestory windows illuminate the stairway and second floor study space, which opens to a full bath and two bedrooms.

Main floor — 1,176 sq. ft.
Second floor — 635 sq. ft.
Width — 28'-0"
(plus 8' of walkway)
Depth — 42'-0" (plus 8' deck)

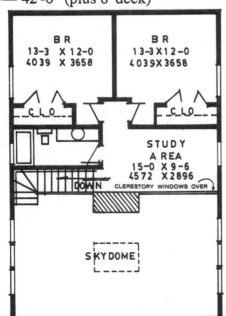

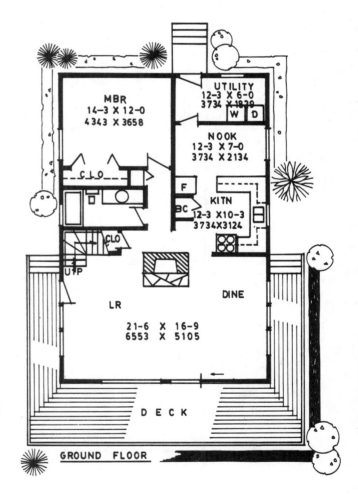

Total living area — 1,811 sq. ft.

Open Floor Plan
Enhances Home

No. 90307

The fireside room of this unique plan features a built-in sofa and opens onto both the kitchen and the dining room. Enclosed in glass and featuring the fireplace for which it is named, this room is designed to be the focal point of the home. The one-walled kitchen and its island are centrally located to accommodate any number of activities. The entry deck and the patio area off the dining room provide facilities for informal meals or outdoor parties. The single bedroom is located on the second level and incorporates its own bump-out window to fill with plants. An inviting sitting room completes this compact plan.

First floor — 768 sq. ft.
Second floor — 419 sq. ft.

Total living area — 1,187 sq. ft.

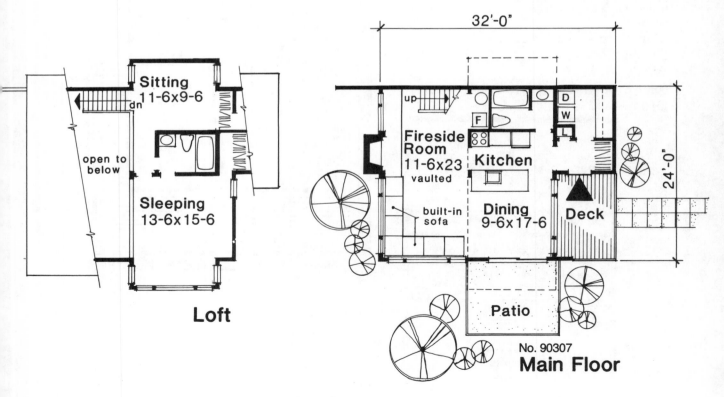

Loft

Sitting 11-6x9-6

dn

open to below

Sleeping 13-6x15-6

32'-0"

24'-0"

up

Fireside Room 11-6x23 vaulted

built-in sofa

Kitchen

D
W
F

Dining 9-6x17-6

Deck

Patio

No. 90307
Main Floor

Build in Stages

No. 90638

With this plan, you can build in stages. In Stage One, a living dining area with a 13 foot cathedral ceiling, sliding glass doors, a climate controlling roof overhang, and a generous deck give you a house that looks and feels luxurious. A prefabricated fireplace covered with decorative stone is designed to circulate heat. A second set of sliding glass doors leads from the efficient L-shaped kitchen onto the deck, making cookouts a snap. And in a one bedroom house you will have four separate closets. Built in either Stage One or Stage Two, a utility storage area off the deck comes with a frame for solar panels to heat water. In Stage Two, add two additional spacious bedrooms and a full bath. The Stage Three carport can be built as funds become available. With this plan, it isn't necessary to wait for good living. This plan is available with a crawl space foundation only.

Stage one — 700 sq. ft.
Stage two — 342 sq. ft.

Total living area — 1,042 sq. ft.

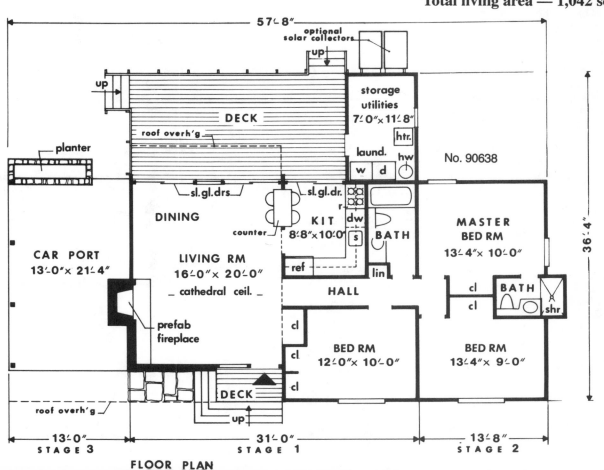

FLOOR PLAN

When There's a Hill

No. 90633

Designed for a site that slopes down, this house is two stories at the entrance, three in the rear. An umbrella roof protects windows from weather and too much sun. The main level, thrusting out over the lower floor, creates a sheltered patio which is further shaded by an L-shaped deck reached through sliding door in an almost all glass wall. The dining room also is lit by two skylights. On the upper level, the master bedroom has a private balcony, deck and bath, and another room can be either bedroom or sitting room. There is, on the lower level, a third bedroom and bath. In fact, each level of this unique hill house has its own full bath. This plan is available with a basement foundation only.

Main level — 790 sq. ft.
Upper level — 453 sq. ft.
Lower level — 340 sq. ft.

Total living area — 1,583 sq. ft.

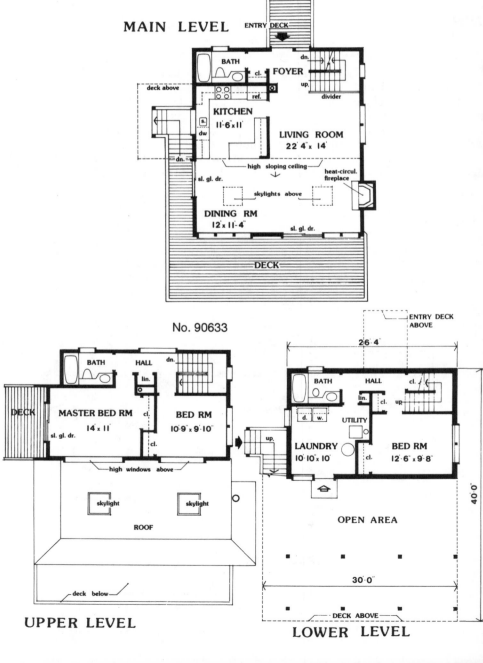

No. 90633

MAIN LEVEL

UPPER LEVEL

LOWER LEVEL

Just the Right Size

No. 90524

You won't find any stairs in this gracious home for a retired couple, but you will find all the necessities you require. Two full bathrooms, for example, reward you with the privacy you've earned as well as make it easier to receive company. You'll find a spacious central entry, a fireplace for comfort and charm, an attached garage for security, a lovely patio directly off the dining room, and full laundry services just steps away. All these useful features are wrapped inside a distinctive home with the exterior stone work and Tudor windows of an English country home.

Main living area — 1,243 sq. ft.
Garage — 2 car

Total living area — 1,243 sq. ft.

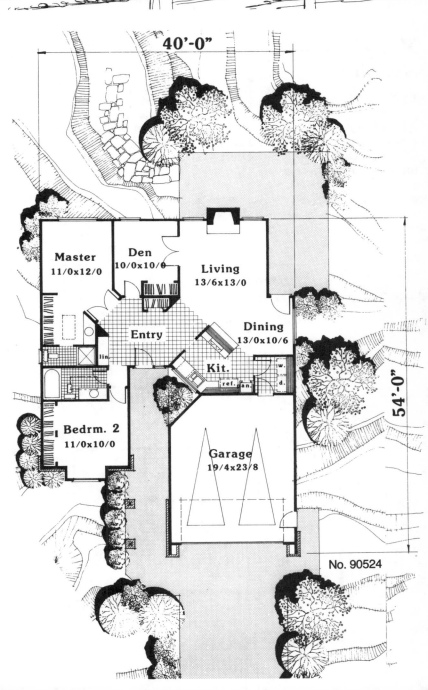

40'-0"

Master 11/0x12/0

Den 10/0x10/0

Living 13/6x13/0

Entry

Dining 13/0x10/6

Kit.

ref. pan.

w. d.

lin.

Bedrm. 2 11/0x10/0

Garage 19/4x23/8

54'-0"

No. 90524

Well-Planned Saltbox Has Rustic Charm

No. 84058

Efficient use of living space creates a spacious feeling in this home perfect for a lakeside location. The living/dining area occupies more than half of the lower level while the balcony overlooking the living area affords an expansive illusion. The central chimney will accommodate a built-in fireplace. The fully-equipped bath adjoins two liberal bedrooms on the upper level. Available in slab, crawl, and basement foundation options.

First floor — 779 sq. ft.
Second floor — 519 sq. ft.
Garage — 300 sq. ft.

Total living area — 1,298 sq. ft.

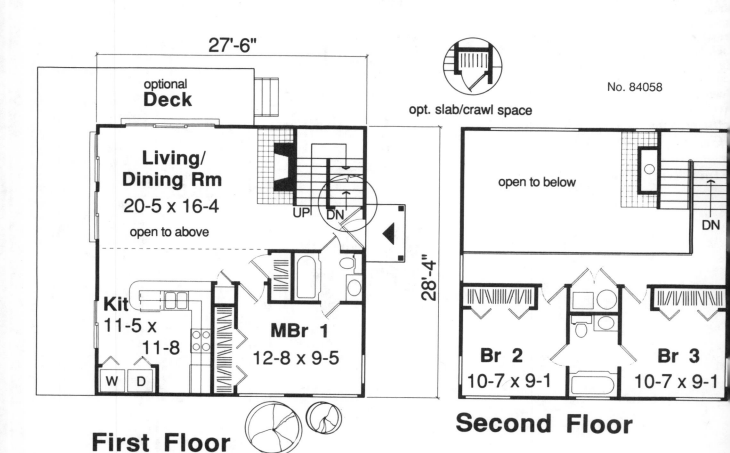

27'-6"

optional
Deck

Living/ Dining Rm
20-5 x 16-4
open to above

UP DN

Kit
11-5 x 11-8

W D

MBr 1
12-8 x 9-5

28'-4"

opt. slab/crawl space

No. 84058

open to below

DN

Br 2
10-7 x 9-1

Br 3
10-7 x 9-1

First Floor

Second Floor

Rustic Charm in This Comfortable Cottage

No. 90855

The rustic charm of this comfortable cottage will make you feel right at home, providing you with hours of relaxing living. Large sundecks across the front of this home yield ample space for outdoor living in good weather. The vaulted ceiling over the sunken living and dining rooms and the stone fireplace are just two of the special features.

Main floor — 1,186 sq. ft.

Width — 41'-0"

Depth — 40'-0"

Total living area — 1,186 sq. ft.

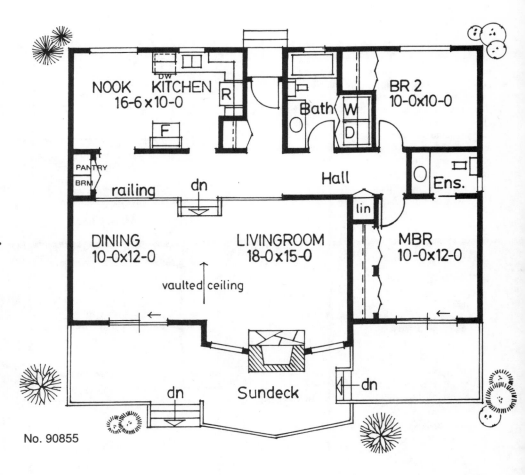

NOOK
KITCHEN
16-6 x 10-0

PANTRY

BRM

railing

dn

BR 2
10-0x10-0

Bath

W

D

Hall

Ens.

lin

DINING
10-0x12-0

LIVINGROOM
18-0x15-0

MBR
10-0x12-0

vaulted ceiling

dn

Sundeck

dn

No. 90855

Leisure Time Getaway

No. 24308

The A-frame's steep roof is designed to shrug off the deep snowfall of a mountain environment, yet, this cabin would be equally at home in any vacation setting. Although this is not a large home, a spacious feeling is achieved by the large open living room. From the living room you can enjoy the outdoors even from inside your home by absorbing the view through all the glass that is the front of the home. Or spend your leisure hours sipping a refreshing cool drink on your deck in the warmer weather while you view nature at its best. Retirement here would make living easy. Your bedroom, kitchen and storage is all on one floor. Yet, that spiral staircase will take you up to the loft for either more sleeping area or hobby space. Whether accompanying the pounding surf of the ocean or the cool mountain air, you may find the simplicity of this A-frame to be just what you are looking for.

First floor — 660 sq. ft.
Loft — 180 sq. ft.

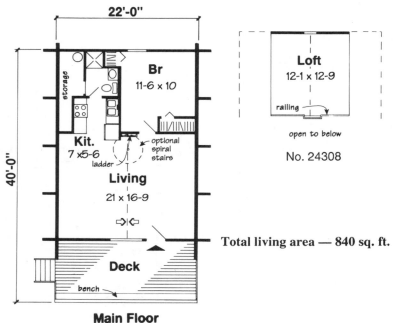

Total living area — 840 sq. ft.

No. 24308

Main Floor

A Pleasure to Own

No. 90821

Relax and enjoy this trouble-free vacation home. With huge expanses of glass to take advantage of beautiful vistas and solar warmth, the vaulted ceilings and an open plan lend a spacious air to a compact design. You'll find living, dining, and kitchen fit comfortably on the main floor with a bedroom and full bath. Tucked upstairs, the roomy loft bedroom boasts a view of the backyard. And, there's lots of storage space under the eaves.

Main floor — 616 sq. ft.
Loft — 199 sq. ft.
Width — 22'-0"
Depth — 28'-0"

Total living area — 815 sq. ft.

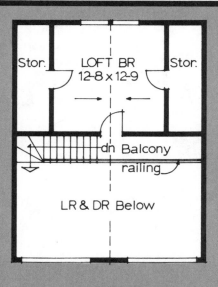

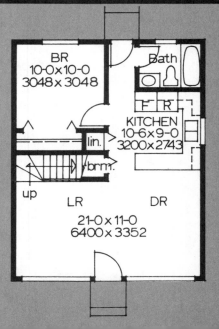

No. 90821

No Time To Waste

No. 24313

All year long you are looking for ways to make your use of time more efficient. When you're on vacation you're there to relax and enjoy yourself. This home was designed to help you do just that. The open living room and kitchen area are cozy and can both enjoy the glowing fireplace in the colder weather. The first floor bedroom is located near the full bath. Upstairs in the loft, you may wish to set up a studio or hobby area. There is also a second bedroom located on this floor with two closets and a bath with shower. The deck is accessed from the living room to expand your living area to the great outdoors. It is all here, all you have to do is enjoy your vacation.

Main floor — 647 sq. ft.
Upper floor — 450 sq. ft.

Total living area — 1,097 sq. ft.

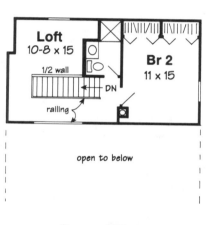

Second Floor

Loft
10-8 x 15

1/2 wall

railing

DN

Br 2
11 x 15

open to below

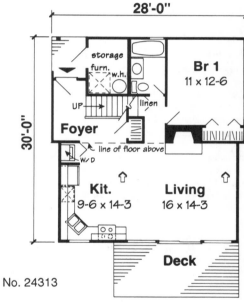

28'-0"

30'-0"

storage
furn.
w.h.
UP
linen
Foyer
W/D
line of floor above
Br 1
11 x 12-6
Kit.
9-6 x 14-3
Living
16 x 14-3
Deck

No. 24313

First Floor

Let the Good Times Roll

No. 90067

Forget all about giving up your privacy on vacation. Here's a house that separates living and sleeping areas with a covered promenade that connects to an expansive deck. In the living area, lit from above by a skylight, you'll find a fireplaced living room, full bath, and large kitchen with a glass-walled eating nook and breakfast bar. Across the quiet promenade, rest well in the three-bedroom skylit unit with full bath. Look at the closet space in this area. There's room for everyone's vacation necessities.

Living unit — 648 sq. ft.
Bedroom unit — 648 sq. ft.

Total living area — 1,296 sq. ft.

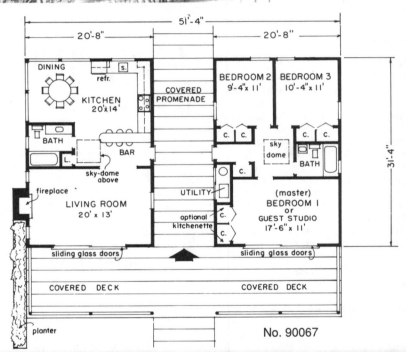

At Home by the Shore or in the Suburbs

No. 90681

This one-and-a-half story home offers contemporary living on a compact scale. Use the loft in this spacious, two-bedroom home as a studio, extra sleeping space, or a private hideaway with a spectacular view. Sliding glass doors unite the fireplaced living room with a wrap-around deck that doubles outdoor living space. And, the convenient pass-through window to the kitchen makes eating on the deck an inviting alternative to the glass-walled dining area. Two bedrooms at the rear of the house are served by a full bath just across the hall. And, if you've chosen a beachfront location for this affordable home, you'll appreciate the shower and dressing room that keep the sand where it belongs. This plan is available with a crawl space foundation only.

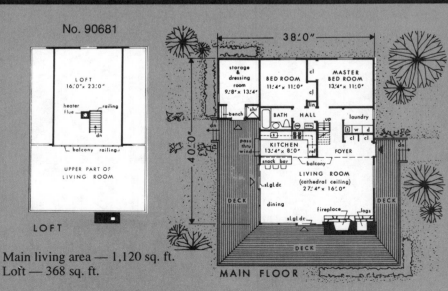

Main living area — 1,120 sq. ft.
Loft — 368 sq. ft.

Total living area — 1,488 sq. ft.

Get Out the Telescope

No. 90066

This classic A-frame has been adapted for your outdoor enjoyment. Two upper-level decks let you take advantage of vacation views in two directions. Walk across the balcony overlooking the lounge and dining area below to a third bedroom with its own covered porch. On the first floor, a huge porch off the fireplaced lounge gives you even more outdoor living space. Past the kitchen, two bedrooms and a full bath share the rear of the house. And, for beach combers with sandy feet, there's a shower in the mudroom, just inside the back door.

First floor — 1,155 sq. ft.
Second floor — 306 sq. ft.

Total living area — 1,461 sq. ft.

second floor plan   No. 90066

Cozy And Spacious

No. 99709

A gambrel, or barn-shaped roofline, and redwood siding give this three-story home the look of a cabin. On the main level, open beams stretching up the side walls and to the peak of the high vaulted-ceiling of the living room bring the cabin flavor inside. Most shared activities will take place in the Great room on this level. Due to the inward sloping interior walls created by the exterior roofline, the kitchen counter along the outside wall is exceptionally deep. Sliding glass doors in the dining room open onto a wide deck. A luxurious master suite fills the entire upper level, while two additional bedrooms, a bathroom and a large family room occupy the basement space below. Wide hearths at the far end of both the family room and living room offer warmth. Exposed beams also grace the walls and ceilings of the master suite. The sleeping room is separated from the high ceiling of the living room by nothing more than a wide balcony railing which stretches along the widest edge of the sleeping area.

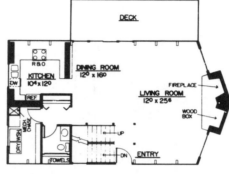

MAIN LEVEL

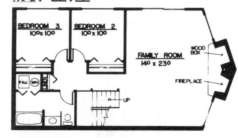

BASEMENT LEVEL

Main level — 912 sq. ft.
Second level — 504 sq. ft.
Lower level — 912 sq. ft.

Total living area — 2,328 sq. ft.

UPPER LEVEL

No. 99709

Cabin With A Gambrel

No. 99701

Bright and cozy, this is a cabin with a gambrel, or barn-styled roof and an open-beam ceiling. Six huge windows brighten a Great room that occupies the front half of the home. Open to the roof beams, this combined living room, dining room and kitchen has a wide open feeling that invites you to shuck off the cares of the world, settle into an easy chair and relax. A woodstove could be included in either the dining or living room to provide additional warmth and cheer. The kitchen is compact, but has plenty of cupboard and counter space. One of the counter extensions could be outfitted as an eating bar. Total privacy is available in the master suite, the only room upstairs. The suite has a private bathroom and two closets. Additional storage space is behind. Two small bedrooms, another bathroom, and an average size utility room are below, at the back of the cabin.

Main floor — 864 sq. ft.
Second floor — 396 sq. ft.

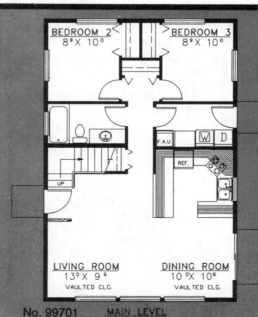

No. 99701   MAIN LEVEL

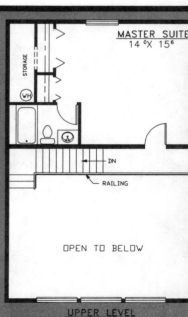

UPPER LEVEL

Total living area — 1,260 sq. ft.

Sunny Cabin

No. 99702

This home's windows and glass sliding doors allows for natural light to flow into the main living areas. The wrap around deck increases living space and allows you to enjoy your surroundings. The living room and dining room feature an open layout. The wood stove in the living room provides a cozy atmosphere and added warmth to the home. The modern kitchen is efficiently layed out for easy meal preparation. The secondary bedrooms are located on this floor. Both are a good size and have ample closet space. They have easy access to a full bath in the hallway. There is also a half bath on this floor. Upstairs offers privacy to the master suite, with a walk-in closet and its own master bath.

Main floor — 1,012 sq. ft.
Second floor — 362 sq. ft.
Garage — 576 sq. ft.

Total living area — 1,374 sq. ft.

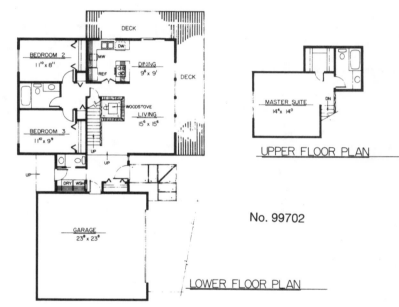

No. 99702

UPPER FLOOR PLAN

LOWER FLOOR PLAN

Swiss Chalet Styled A-Frame

No. 99707

With its A-frame roofline echoed in the diamond-shaped mullioned windows and decorative railings, this home instantly puts one in mind of the Swiss chalet. The steep roof is designed to shrug off the deep snowfall of high altitude environments with ease. The living room, dining room and kitchen all flow together, unimpaired by structural impediments. The kitchen is larger than in most small cabins, and includes a pantry, and a washer and dryer. The upper floor, with its steeply pitched, open-beamed ceiling, can be put to many uses. Narrower than the lower floor, it is still quite wide with a 16-foot width of usable space. A wide balcony stretches across the full width of the upper floor.

Main floor — 864 sq. ft.
Second floor — 612 sq. ft.

Total living area — 1,476 sq. ft.

No. 99707

FIRST FLOOR PLAN

BEDROOM
9⁴ X 11⁶

DINING
9⁰ X 9⁰

PANTRY

FIREPLACE

UP

DN

DN

LIVING AREA
23⁴ X 18⁰

DN

DECK

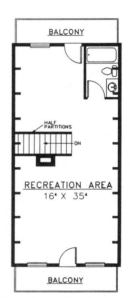

SECOND FLOOR PLAN

BALCONY

HALF PARTITIONS

DN

RECREATION AREA
16⁴ X 35⁴

BALCONY

Homey Simplicity

No. 99708

Step from a covered porch into a wide entry-way. The living room, dining room and kitchen are on the right side of the house. The bedroom and baths comprise the left side. Each bedroom features its own bath and yards of closet space. This arrangement works out nicely when another couple or other friends visit. The kitchen features a U-shaped set-up with everything within arm's reach. Have breakfast at the eating bar, or layout the festive board in the dining room. The nearby pantry stands ready if you want to lay in stores for the winter. The home features open-beam vaulted-ceilings throughout.

Main living area — 1,162 sq. ft.
Garage — 576 sq. ft.

Total living area — 1,162 sq. ft.

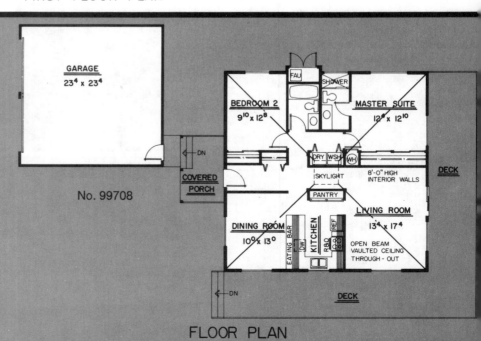

GARAGE
23⁴ x 23⁴

No. 99708

COVERED PORCH

DN

FLOOR PLAN

BEDROOM 2
9¹⁰ x 12⁸

MASTER SUITE
12⁸ x 12¹⁰

FAU

SHOWER

DRY WSH WH

SKYLIGHT

8'-0" HIGH INTERIOR WALLS

DECK

PANTRY

LIVING ROOM
13⁴ x 17⁴

DINING ROOM
10⁹ x 13⁰

EATING BAR

DW

KITCHEN

BBQ

REF

OPEN BEAM VAULTED CEILING THROUGH - OUT

DECK

DN

DECK

For Year-Round Recreational Use

No. 91725

This cabin, designed for year-round recreational use, has a long sun porch, complete with sink, stretching across most of the back of the cabin. When temperatures climb into the comfort zone and beyond, a wide deck nearly doubles the available living area. The sturdy woodstove pumps out enough heat to keep the cabin cozy. The kitchen is surprisingly large and seems even larger because it is completely open to the lofty dining and living room. The first floor bathroom is compartmentalized, with the toilet and and oversize shower separate from the lavatory. Access is from two sides — through the utility room, or the living room. Upstairs, a bathroom with a tub, serves the two narrow bedrooms. A large linen closet fills the space in front of the stairs, at the landing.

First floor — 1,040 sq. ft.
Second floor — 383 sq. ft.

Total living area — 1,423 sq. ft.

No. 91725

Which Will it Be?

No. 90824

Eliminate the basement, carport, and storage area of this design, and you have a low-cost vacation home. Build it as shown, and you have an attractive and practical year-round residence. You choose when and how to complete the plan. All the rooms are larger than average. There are plenty of closets throughout. The spectacular vaulted ceiling and balcony hall accentuate the exceptional roominess of these spaces. Downstairs there is a master bedroom and full bath, upstairs three more bedrooms, another full bath, and the balconied hall. In this home, everyone will appreciate your choice.

Main floor — 1,008 sq. ft.
Second floor — 612 sq. ft.
Width — 40'-8"
Depth — 42'-0"

Total living area — 1,620 sq. ft.

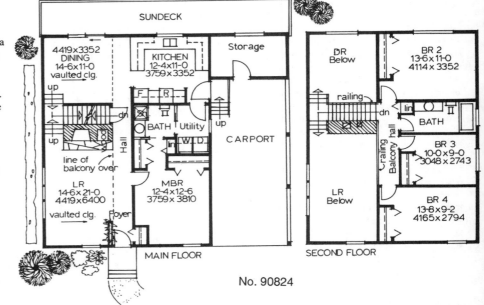

No. 90824

For That View Of The Lake

No. 24310

For the view of the ocean, or the view of the slopes, look at the glass and imagine how you would place this home on your scenic lot to take full advantage of the view. Almost one entire wall of the living room is made up of glass. The center fireplace is circular, adding warmth and a focal point to the room. The dining and kitchen area flow off of this room. There is one bedroom on this floor and a studio area upstairs that could also be a secondary bedroom. The wrap-around deck makes it easy to enjoy your surroundings. The dining room also accesses the deck to make outdoor meals convenient.

First floor — 600 sq. ft.
Loft — 240 sq. ft.

Total living area — 840 sq. ft.

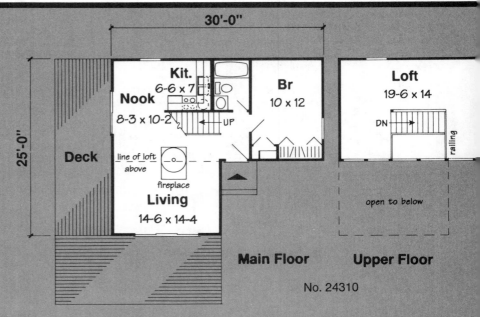

No. 24310

Spacious Simplicity

No. 24312

This contemporary styled home gives you style, yet keeps things uncomplicated. The spacious living room features wood burning stove or fireplace. The efficent kitchen is larger than what is usually found in a vacation home and features an area of counter that can be used as an eating bar. The gourmet of your family may not want to take a vacation from his duties in this kitchen. There is a bedroom on this floor and two bedrooms and a bath upstairs providing privacy to all. One of the upstairs bedroom features a deck all its own. Storage is not a problem here with ample closets and a storage area. In the future this second home may provide a fantastic retirement residence.

First floor — 840 sq. ft.
Second floor — 442 sq. ft.

Total living area — 1,282 sq. ft.

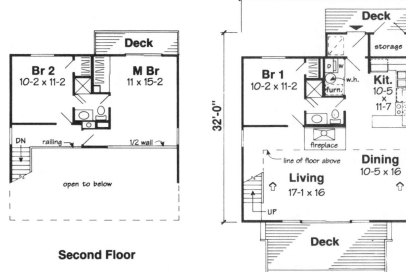

Second Floor

No. 24312

First Floor

Designed For Sloping Lot

No. 99704

This floor plan is designed for construction on a lot that slopes down at the back and to the left. All the family living space is on the main floor, the portion of the home that's visible from the street. But there's a full daylight basement below. One section of it is a garage and workshop. A wide deck wraps around three sides of the home, inviting outdoor living when the weather permits and offering multiple vistas to the left and the rear. The living room is also richly windowed to take advantage of these same views. The far end of the room is warm and bright, with skylights providing additional illumination and a woodstove radiating heat during the chilly seasons. The large country kitchen faces out toward an eating area expanded and brightened by a bay window. An eating bar provides separation and, doubles as a buffet on special occasions. The bedrooms are clustered together. The master suite has a bay window, private bath and large walk-in closet. One of the other two bedrooms also has a walk-in closet.

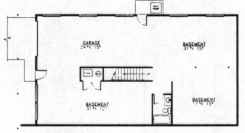

BASEMENT PLAN

Main living area — 1,824 sq. ft
Basement — 1,258 sq. ft.
Garage — 496 sq. ft.

Total living area — 1,824 sq.

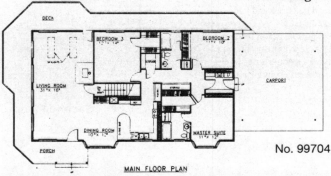

MAIN FLOOR PLAN

No. 99704

Expandable Design

No. 91751

Windows fill most of the front facade, creating an open look, while gales and a wide front porch amplify the effect. A ramp provides wheelchair accessibility and inner doors are also wide. Everything an average family needs is on the 2,200 sq. ft. main floor. If more living space is required now, or later, another 1,000 sq. ft. can be developed upstairs. The optional second floor plan adds three bedrooms, two of them quite large, and compartmentalized bathroom. Family living is at the heart, a comfortably sized kitchen/family room. Secondary bedrooms are to the left and quiet rooms, living room and owners' suite, are on the right, well-isolated from the everyday commotion. The kitchen is bright and spacious with lots of windows.

Main floor plan — 2,199 sq. ft.
Optional second floor plan — 999 sq. ft.
Covered porch — 462 sq. ft.

Basement — 2,199 sq. ft.
Garage — 606 sq. ft.
Storage — 72 sq. ft.

Total living area — 3,198 sq. ft.

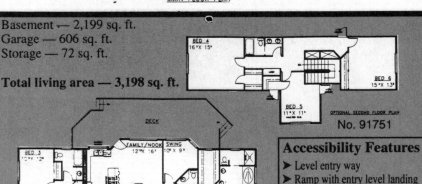

No. 91751

Accessibility Features

- ➤ Level entry way
- ➤ Ramp with entry level landing
- ➤ Wide doorways (32"-36" clear width)
- ➤ Low-pile carpeting with thin padding
- ➤ Chair-height electrical controls/outlets
- ➤ Direct outside emergency exit from bedroom in some cases
- ➤ Reinforced walls (i.e. 3/4" plywood backing throughout) for installation of grab bars

Contemporary Cabin

No. 99706

In this contemporary cabin, windows in all of the living areas face toward the back of the home to take full advantage of a vista. The central high-vaulted hexagonal Great room has open beams and combines the functions of kitchen, dining room and living room. The woodstove, seated on a wide hexagonal hearth at its center, provides a warm focal point for this bright airy and spacious central living room. A modified U-shaped kitchen is separated from the rest of the room by nothing more than an eating bar. A utility room, complete with a utility sink and a wide counter, is conveniently located next to the kitchen, with a huge walk-in pantry right next door. Two rectangular areas on nearly opposite sides of the hexagon house the sleeping areas, offering privacy to both. The master suite has a double-sided walk-in closet and twin vanities located outside the bathroom. Sliding doors here, and in the dining room, open onto a wide wrap-around deck.

Main living area — 2,193 sq. ft.
Garage — 546 sq. ft.

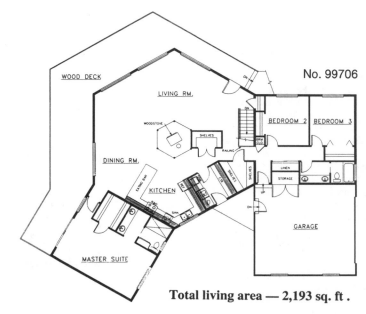

Total living area — 2,193 sq. ft .

A Plan with Lofty Ideas

No. 21120

An attractive beginning for this home is found in the centrally located foyer. Down several steps lies a sunken family room, accentuated by two stories of glass at its rear, cathedral ceiling and a fireplace. The family room shares openness of design with the adjacent kitchen and dining room. Stairs spiral from the foyer to a second level loft which overlooks the family room below from a full length balcony and accesses a private exterior deck through glass doors on the other side. A master bedroom with its own bath lies secluded to the left of the foyer. An additional bath and washer-dryer facilities are located off the hall to the master suite. A carport, 49 square feet of storage at its rear and a covered terrace, accessed from the kitchen and family room, complete the plan. No materials list available for this plan.

First floor — 947 sq. ft.
Second floor — 232 sq. ft.
Carport — 346 sq. ft.
Storage — 49 sq. ft.
Total living area — 1,179 sq. ft.

No materials list available

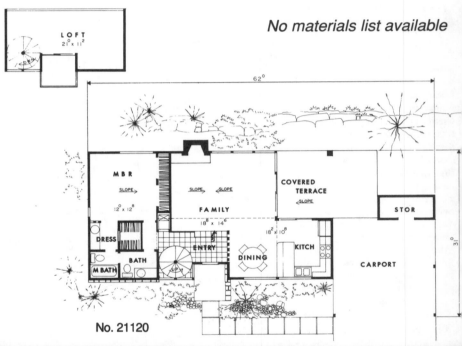

No. 21120

Energy Efficient and Compact

No. 21122

This compact dwelling is simple but organized and efficient. The open floor plan calls for a kitchen, dining room, and living room area unbroken by walls. All ceilings in the design slope to a peak above this open area. Fixed glass has been placed in every nook and cranny left by the sloping ceilings and, together with abundant sun-catching windows, adds an energy saving feature. The massive stone fireplace and wood storage bin attract your eye in the living room. Two bedrooms, a full bath and a carport are located to the right of the plan. A storage area, which also houses the washer-dryer facilities and water heater, can be accessed from the carport. A large deck lies to the rear of the home. No materials list available for this plan.

Main living area — 1,062 sq. ft.
Carport — 242 sq. ft.
Storage — 77 sq. ft

No materials list available

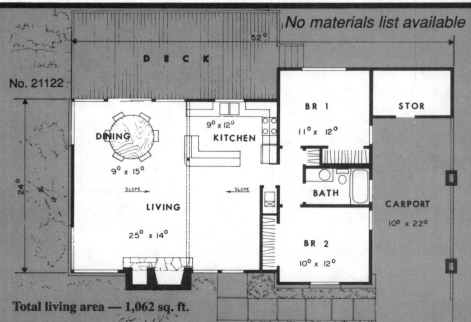

No. 21122

Total living area — 1,062 sq. ft.

English Tudor Influence

No. 26002

This dramatic Tudor styled home welcomes you into a large foyer at the front door. A cathedral beamed ceiling in the living room with a built-in fireplace in the corner creates a cozy atmosphere for the family. Large bay windows flood the dining room with sunlight and in the evening, starlight. Adjacent to the kitchen is a screened porch inviting outdoor entertaining. The open stairway in the living room leads to the second floor culminating in a dramatic view of the living room from the balcony. There are two bedrooms and a bath upstairs with an additional 11 x 14 storage room. Two bedrooms and two baths are on the first floor, providing plenty of room for a growing family.

First floor — 1,312 sq. ft.
Second floor — 698 sq. ft.
Family room/basement — 508 sq. ft.
Basement — 679 sq. ft.
Garage — 483 sq. ft.

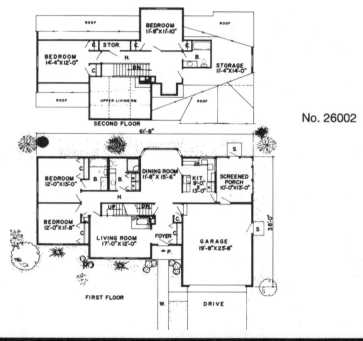

No. 26002

Total living area — 2,110 sq. ft.

Be in Tune with the Elements

No. 24240

Designed to work with nature, not against it, this simple design will allow you to be in tune with the elements. Instead of being sealed up in your home, the breezes flow from front to back, heat rising to the attic, cool air settling. The cozy living room has a fireplace. There is a formal dining room and a modern, efficient kitchen with a booth set aside for less formal eating. The master bedroom has a private bath and there is a full bath in the hallway. The second bedroom is a nice size with ample closet space. There are two covered porches. Maybe you will put a big swing on the front porch. So you can sit and swing, feeling the warm summer breeze, and listening to distant thunder of a summer storm.
Main living area — 964 sq. ft.

Total living area — 964 sq. ft.

No. 24240

Main Floor

Modified A-Frame

No. 99705

This modified A-frame is a vacation cabin that looks right at home nestled under tall trees or along the shore of a beach or lake. Its design, with mirror-image bedrooms, located on opposite sides of the central living area, lends itself easily to dual ownership. Windows sparkle across most of the front of this home, drawing admiring glances from passers-by, while flooding the interior with soft, natural light. The shape of the front deck reflects the A-shaped peak above. A screened or glassed-in sun porch makes equally good use of the light along the back of the house. An artist would love this room. The porch is flanked on both sides by matching garages. The kitchen is large, with an eating bar, pantry and dishwasher. Built-in utilities are tucked behind sliding doors in the nearby half-bath. The living room vaulted to the ceiling can enjoy warm breezes through the sliding glass doors of the

deck. Both bedrooms also have access to the deck. The loft upstairs is a bonus area.
Main living area — 2,091 sq. ft.
Garage — 742 sq. ft.

Total living area — 2,091 sq. ft.

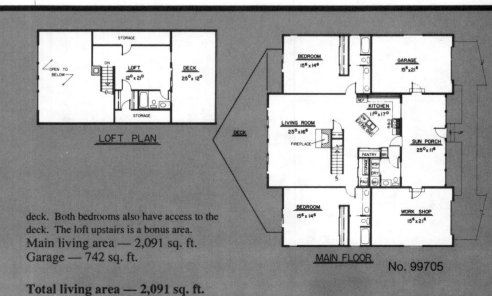

LOFT PLAN

MAIN FLOOR   No. 99705

Designed for the TV Buff

No. 90621

No matter where you decide to build, you'll be sure to get perfect TV reception in the living room of this passive solar home. A satellite dish shares south-facing roof space with skylights and hot water solar collectors. The entertainment center is visible from all the living areas, grouped together in an open space. The entrance foyer leads to the main rooms and the master bedroom off the bathroom hall. The upstairs hall, two bedrooms, and bath are brightened by clerestory windows. With energy-saving construction features, this home will give you years of enjoyment with minimal energy costs.

First floor (excluding deck) — 967 sq. ft.

Second floor — 389 sq. ft.

Total living area — 1,356 sq. ft.

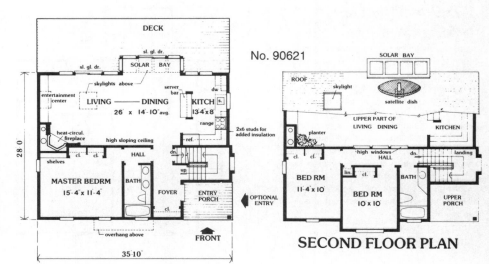

No. 90621

FIRST FLOOR PLAN

SECOND FLOOR PLAN

A Tudor-Style Gem

No. 90172

A private, sheltered stairway leads to your comfortable retreat over this two-car garage plan. Designed to provide secure storage for recreational vehicles or boats while you're away, these plans are becoming increasingly popular thanks to their affordability and style. Beautifully designed, the living space includes room for washer and dryer, a full bath with tub, a handy kitchen, an optional deck off the dining area, a separate entry space, surprisingly roomy living room, and good-sized bedroom. Tudor accents on the exterior lend a touch of class to a structure that will give you peace of mind while you're away.

Main living area — 784 sq. ft.
Garage — 784 sq. ft.

Total living area — 784 sq. ft.

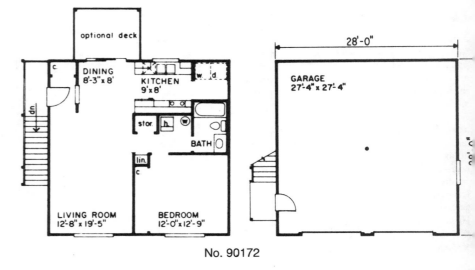

No. 90172

Quiet Summer Hide-A-Way

No. 24241

A beautiful bungalow home with an exceptionally attractive and convenient interior arrangement. The covered porch welcomes you. As you enter into the fireplaced living room, to your left is the dining room with built-in china cabinet. The kitchen efficiently uses its space with ample cabinets, counters and even a pantry. The master bedroom boasts a private bath. The two secondary bedrooms share a full hallway bath. This typical bungalow design allows for rising heat to collect in the attic space, keeping the house cool. A perfect summer hide-a-way.

Main living area — 1,172 sq. ft.

Total living area — 1,172 sq. ft.

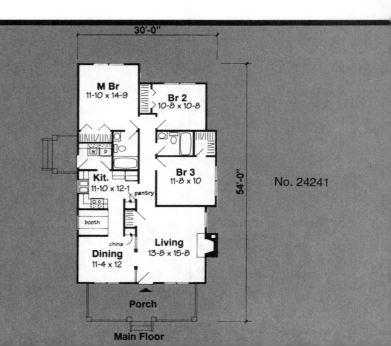

No. 24241

Savor the Summer

No. 24242

This attractive bungalow home with an inviting covered porch, can accommodate a large family. With not one foot of wasted space, this four bedroom home is the perfect habitation for the summer months. The efficient kitchen offers an eating booth, ample cabinet and counter space and all the modern conveniences to make meal preparation a snap. The master bedroom lets you have your privacy from the kids, it also boasts ample closet space and a private bath. The living room has a cozy fireplace and a bright, bay window. There is even a formal dining area. Upstairs the three secondary bedrooms share a full bath. Sip your cool drink, enjoy a summer breeze as you relax on your covered porch and savor the summer.

First floor — 920 sq. ft.
Second floor — 624 sq. ft.

Total living area — 1,544 sq. ft.

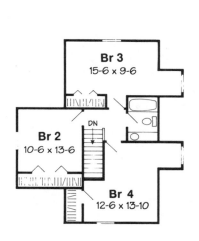

Br 3
15-6 x 9-6

Br 2
10-6 x 13-6

DN

Br 4
12-6 x 13-10

Second Floor

No. 24242

30'-0"

40'-0"

M Br
14-8 x 12-6

Kitchen
10-9 x 9-10

Dining
10-9 x 10

Living
11-6 x 14-10

DN

UP

1/2 wall

booth

D
W

seat

Porch

First Floor

Compact Geodesic Retreat

No. 91101

Here's a cozy vacation home designed for easy living — and, every room has a view. And, you'll love the 30 to 50 percent energy savings you'll realize over a conventional home with the same square footage, thanks to the smaller surface area exposed to the elements. The kitchen and adjacent dining room are designed for simple meal service. There's lots of storage space for extra groceries and all your gear, including a washer and dryer. You'll find a convenient full bath just across from the first-floor bedroom. And, in the two-story living room, soaring ceilings and an open staircase create a light and airy luxurious loft suite, isolated from living areas for maximum privacy.

First floor — 1,439 sq. ft.
Second floor — 873 sq. ft.

Total living area — 2,312 sq. ft.

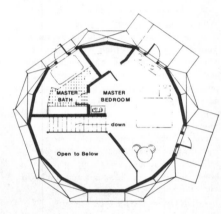

No. 91101

Relaxed and Economical Living

No. 21126

Well suited for the economy-minded small family or as a second home, this design is sure to please. To the left of a large front entry lies the living room, with deck access, a fireplace and a cathedral ceiling with exposed beams. The living room flows through an eating bar to the kitchen-dining area beyond. The dining room also adjoins the deck. To the right of the entry are two bedrooms and a full bath. Sliding glass doors and full-length windows cloak the entire width of the rear of the house on this level. A touch of elegance is provided by a stairway spiraling to the second-floor loft. Clerestory windows draw in the sun and illuminate this quiet, secluded room. No materials list available for this plan.

First floor — 1,082 sq. ft.
Loft — 262 sq. ft.
Total living area — 1,344 sq. ft.

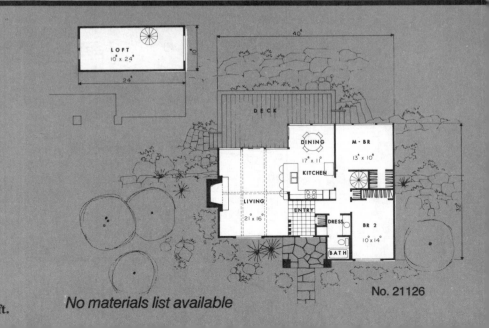

No materials list available

No. 21126

A Family Play House

No. 90169

This plan has everything a family wants on vacation including that all-important second bathroom. Four bedrooms flank a roomy living space that is open to light and air through sliding glass windows on two sides and clerestory windows above. The kitchen area features both an eating counter and table space, and a laundry niche too. Clean and contemporary, without unnecessary frills, this house could be exactly what you're looking for. This plan can be built with a crawl space foundation only.

Main living area — 1,176 sq. ft.

Total living area — 1,176 sq. ft.

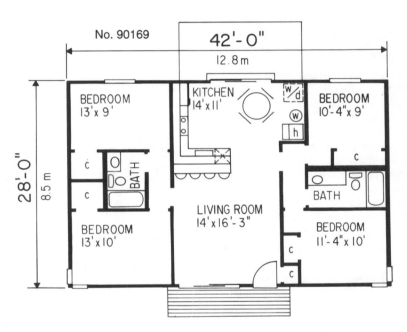

No. 90169

42'-0"
12.8 m

28'-0"
8.5 m

BEDROOM 13' x 9'

KITCHEN 14' x 11'

BEDROOM 10'-4" x 9'

BATH

BATH

BEDROOM 13' x 10'

LIVING ROOM 14' x 16'-3"

BEDROOM 11'-4" x 10'

Villa in the Palms

No. 90525

An all-around overhanging roof provides cooling shade for this one floor villa. Classic touches include the treatment of the tiled entry, kitchen, breakfast nook, and two bathrooms. An attached garage protects cars from sun, while a fireplace takes the chill off winter evenings. A third bedroom can be used as a den. Best of all, a large, three-arched bay window brings light and glamour to the living room of this house with just the right touch of Spain.
Main living area — 1,299 sq. ft.

Total living area — 1,299 sq. ft.

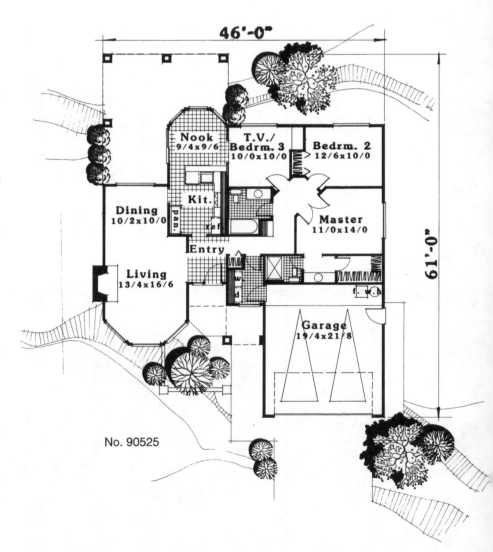

No. 90525

All Year Leisure

No. 90630

Natural materials used inside and out, and good design, make this ranch house easy to build and easy to live in. Three sliding glass doors lead from the living room to a large glass deck. A cathedral ceiling with exposed beams and a stone wall with heat-circulating fireplace give the interior a charming and solid look. A table for informal meals separates the far end of the living room from the kitchen which opens either into the hall or the handy laundry/storage/mudroom inside the back door. Two good sized double bedrooms, a single bedroom, and two full baths complete the bedroom wing. In this house, simplicity is the key. This plan is available in a crawl space foundation only.

Main living area — 1,207 sq. ft. (plus mudroom/laundry and deck)

Total living area — 1,207 sq. ft.

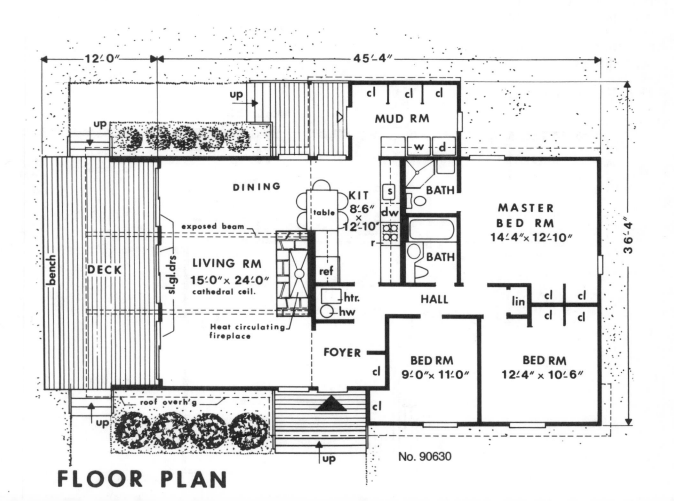

FLOOR PLAN

No. 90630

House with a View

No. 90418

Modest in appearance, this vacation home offers a lot of open living areas. This two-level home has two bedrooms and a bath located on the upper level and another bedroom and bath on the lower level. A kitchen and utility room are located off the living/dining area. This plan is available with a basement, crawl space or slab foundation. Please specify when ordering.

First floor — 1,304 sq. ft.
Second floor — 303 sq. ft.

Total living area — 1,607 sq. ft.

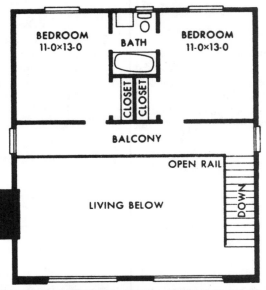

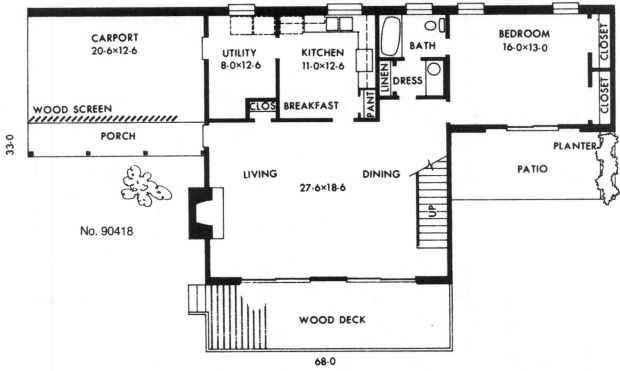

No. 90418

Low Budget Luxury

No. 90631

This contemporary house uses nature's energy and an architect's intelligence for economy with style. The family room/kitchen features a greenhouse sun space and access to a large deck made for relaxed entertaining. Clerestory windows and an attractive bay window bring sunlight and fresh air into the living room which features a prefabricated, heat-circulating fireplace. The master bedroom has its own bath with shower and two closets, one of them a walk-in. Two other bedrooms share a full bath. A laundry is off the attached garage. With this plan, you can save money without sacrificing the benefits of good design.

Main living area — 1,369 sq. ft.
Garage — 220 sq. ft.
Basement — 1,268 sq. ft.

Total living area — 1,589 sq. ft.

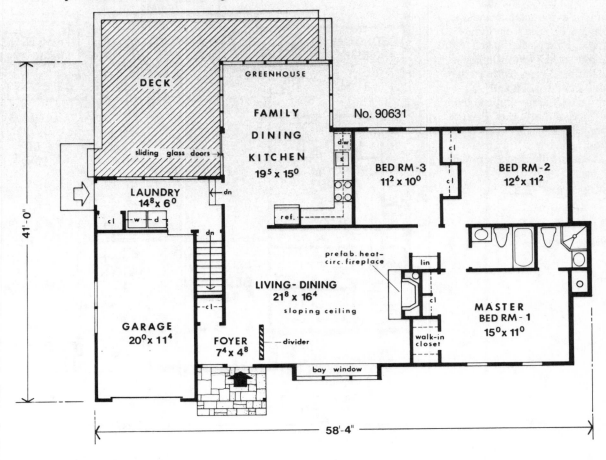

DECK

GREENHOUSE

FAMILY
DINING
KITCHEN
19⁵ x 15⁰

No. 90631

sliding glass doors →

BED RM-3
11² x 10⁰

BED RM-2
12⁶ x 11²

LAUNDRY
14⁸ x 6⁰

cl

cl

← dn

dw

ref.

w d

cl

dn

prefab. heat-
circ. fireplace

lin

cl

41'-0"

GARAGE
20⁰ x 11⁴

LIVING- DINING
21⁸ x 16⁴
sloping ceiling

FOYER
7⁴ x 4⁸

divider

walk-in
closet

MASTER
BED RM- 1
15⁰ x 11⁰

bay window

58'-4"

Central Atrium Highlights Well-Organized Plan

No. 10464

Bring the outdoors in no matter what the season with glass-walled atrium incorporated into this elegant plan. The tiled family room carries out the indoor-outdoor living scheme and open room arrangement. The front living room has a large fireplace flanked with bookcases plus access to the dining room which is easily entered from the kitchen. A breakfast nook and convenient laundry area complete the functional areas of this home. Each of the spacious bedrooms has its own walk-in closet and bath. The master suite has a separate dressing room with five-piece bath.

Main living area—2,222 sq. ft.
Garage—468 sq. ft.

Total living area — 2,222 sq. ft.

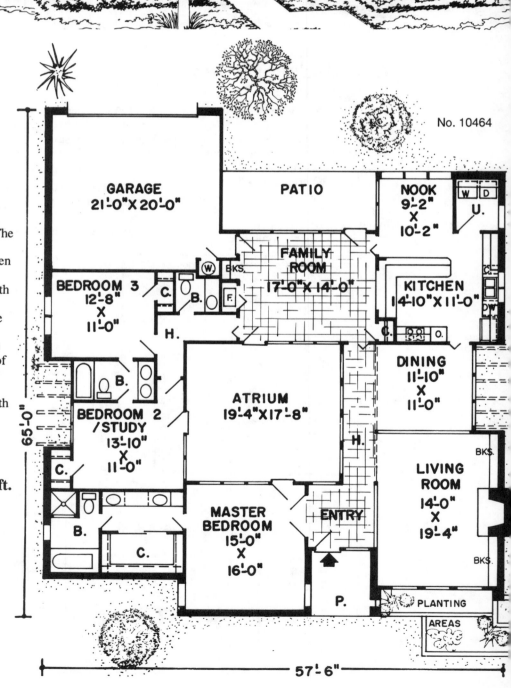

No. 10464

GARAGE 21'-0" X 20'-0"

PATIO

NOOK 9'-2" X 10'-2"

W D U.

FAMILY ROOM 17'-0" X 14'-0"

KITCHEN 14'-10" X 11'-0"

BEDROOM 3 12'-8" X 11'-0"

C. B. W. BKS. F.

DINING 11'-10" X 11'-0"

H.

BEDROOM 2 /STUDY 13'-10" X 11'-0"

ATRIUM 19'-4" X 17'-8"

H.

LIVING ROOM 14'-0" X 19'-4"

BKS.

C.

B.

MASTER BEDROOM 15'-0" X 16'-0"

ENTRY

BKS.

C.

P.

PLANTING AREAS

65'-0"

57'-6"

Enjoy the Outdoors In or Out

No. 90167

With a deck on one side and a dining patio on another, you will never find it too windy or too sunny to enjoy meals outside or open air relaxing. Angled two story window walls bring that joy inside the dramatic living room. Imagine on one side of you a fire in the fireplace, and on the other a view of the stars. Two bedrooms up and two down with super closet space and a storage room, an efficient L-shaped kitchen, and an entrance hall where you can greet your guests, make this home a pleasure to live in.

First floor — 1,186 sq. ft.
Second floor — 692 sq. ft.

Total living area — 1,878 sq. ft.

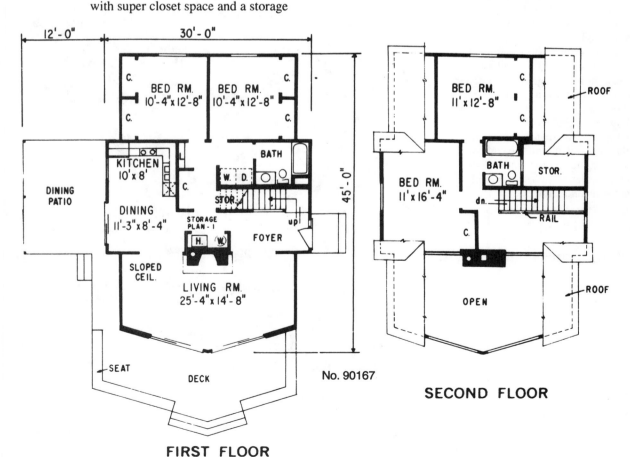

FIRST FLOOR

SECOND FLOOR

Unique One Level Design

No. 91702

This home is a wonderfully unique design allowing for maximum utilization of interior space and a compelling exterior. The impressive living area features extensive oversized windows and sliding glass doors, allowing for a truly panoramic view and taking full advantage of natural light. At the center of this vaulted structure is a six-sided hearth with a central wood stove, which provides separation for the various areas. The dining area is located in the lower angles, abutting the generous kitchen area, which features a breakfast bar. The left wing contains two bedrooms, a full bath with double wash basins, and entry into the two-car garage. The master suite, located in the right wing, contains an impressive walk-in dressing closet and a large bath with double wash basins and vanity.

Main living area — 1,883 sq. ft.
Garage — 484 sq. ft.

Total living area — 1,883 sq. ft.

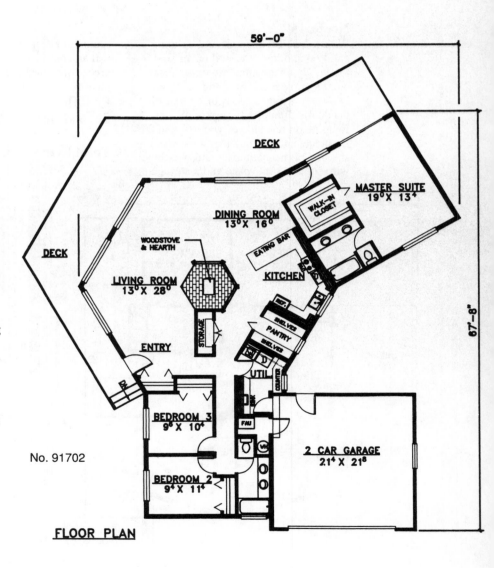

No. 91702

FLOOR PLAN

All On One Floor

No. 92805

This ranch styled home offers you privacy, style, and elegance all on one floor. The master bedroom features a walk-in closet and a private bath. There is a large center fireplace dividing the dining/family area from the living room area. Both these areas are graced with cathedral ceilings and sliding glass doors. The modern kitchen has easy access to the laundry area. The secondary bedrooms are located at the opposite end of the house from the master bedroom providing

privacy to the master bedroom. The secondary bedrooms share a full bath located in the hall and have ample closet space. The dining/family room have access to the wood deck adding living space to the home. One floor convenience, make this home ready for the retired life.

Main living area — 1,768 sq. ft.

Total living area — 1,768 sq. ft.

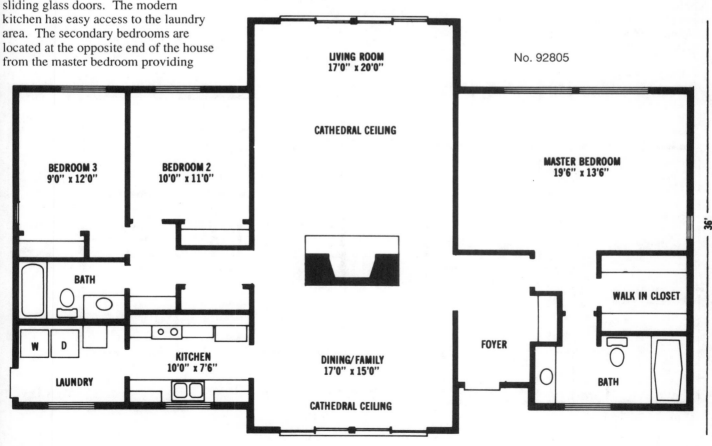

Vacation Fun for Several Families

No. 92807

This home offers an excellent opportunity for added income as a rental property. The four bedrooms give enough room for several families to spread out and have an enjoyable vacation at the beach. The two and a half bathrooms are conveniently located: two full baths upstairs near the bedrooms and a half bath on the first

floor. The kitchen is large, allowing for a few cooks to have enough work space to complete their tasks without getting in each others way. The dining room, living room, and family room flow into each other, appearing larger than they actually are and allowing for easy traffic flow. The living room has access to a wrap-around deck as do two of the bedrooms. This home was designed for a coastal lot, taking full advantage of your view of the water.

First floor — 1,008 sq. ft.
Second floor — 1,024 sq. ft.

Total living area — 2,032 sq. ft.

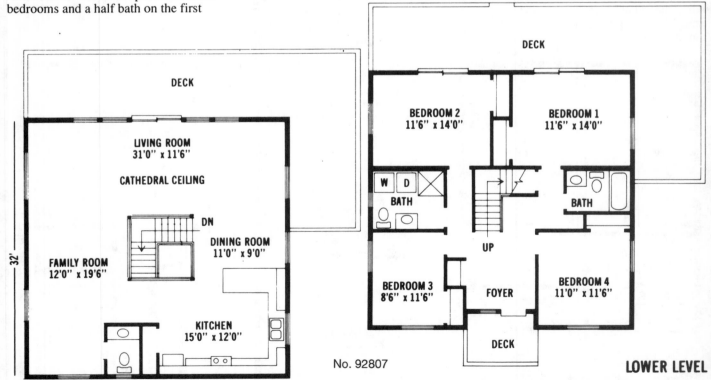

A Home for All Seasons

No. 90629

The natural cedar and stone exterior of this contemporary gem is virtually maintenance free, and its dramatic lines echo the excitement inside. There are so many luxurious touches in this plan: the two-story living room overlooked by an upper-level balcony, a massive stone wall that pierces the roof and holds two fireplaces, a kitchen oven and an outdoor barbecue. Outdoor dining is a pleasure with the barbecue so handy to the kitchen. All the rooms boast outdoor decks, and each bedroom has its own. The front entrance, garage, a dressing room with bath, and laundry room occupy the lower level. This plan is available with a basement foundation only.

Main level — 1,001 sq. ft.
Upper level — 712 sq. ft.
Lower level — 463 sq. ft.

Total living area — 2,176 sq. ft.

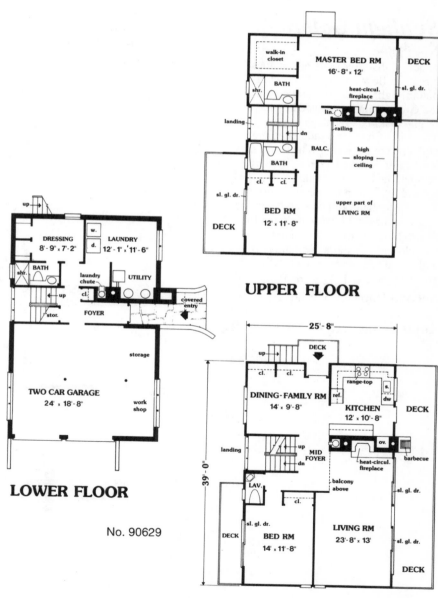

UPPER FLOOR

LOWER FLOOR

No. 90629

MAIN FLOOR

Sunlight Galore

No. 92806

A design that gives lots of spacious, large and flowing areas filled with natural light. The cathedral ceiling in the Great room is enhanced by the use of glass taking advantage of your view. There is a fireplace to add even more ambience to the room. The kitchen/dining area, using a modern, efficient layout also drinks in the natural light from its many windows. The master bedroom enjoys the privacy of being the only bedroom on the first floor. It has its own private bath and two closets. Upstairs there are two additional bedrooms and a full bath.

First floor — 1,323 sq. ft.
Second floor — 518 sq. ft.

Total living area — 1,841 sq. ft.

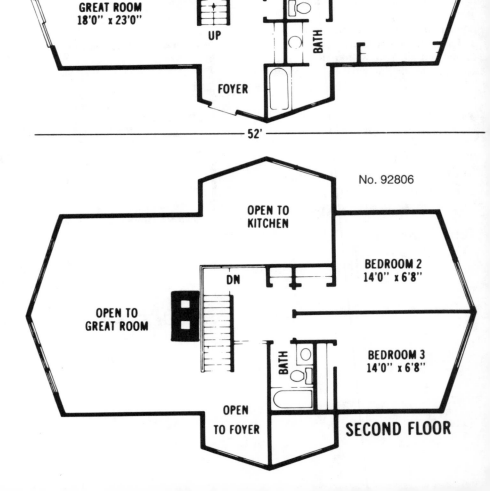

FIRST FLOOR

KITCHEN/DINING
15'0" x 11'0"

CATHEDRAL CEILING

MASTER BEDROOM
14'0" x 18'0"

GREAT ROOM
18'0" x 23'0"

UP

BATH

FOYER

— 52' —

No. 92806

OPEN TO KITCHEN

BEDROOM 2
14'0" x 6'8"

DN

OPEN TO GREAT ROOM

BEDROOM 3
14'0" x 6'8"

BATH

OPEN TO FOYER

SECOND FLOOR

Happy Hill House

No. 91026

Built into a hill, this vacation house takes advantage of your wonderful view. It features a Great room that opens out on a deck and brings earth and sky into the home through sweeping panels of glass. The open plan draws the kitchen into the celebration of the outdoors and shares the warmth of the sturdy wood stove. Two bedrooms on the main level share a bath. Two large, upstairs lofts, one overlooking the Great room, have a full bath all to themselves. This house feels as airy and delightful as a tree house. This plan can be built with a basement foundation only.

Main level — 988 sq. ft.
Upper level — 366 sq. ft.
Basement — 988 sq. ft.

Total living area — 1,354 sq. ft.

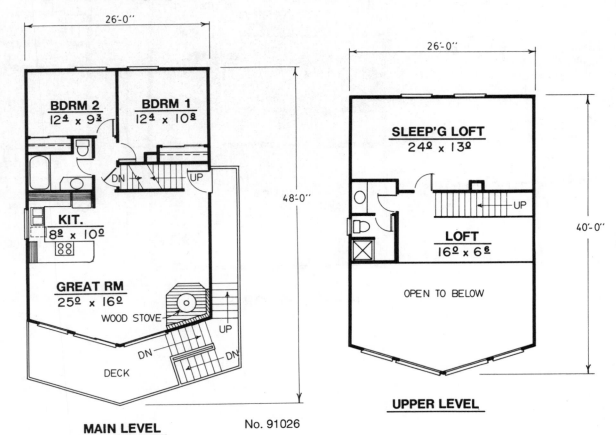

26'-0''

BDRM 2
12⁴ x 9³

BDRM 1
12⁴ x 10⁰

KIT.
8⁰ x 10⁰

GREAT RM
25⁰ x 16⁰

WOOD STOVE

DN

UP

UP

DN

DN

DECK

48'-0''

MAIN LEVEL

No. 91026

26'-0''

SLEEP'G LOFT
24⁰ x 13⁰

UP

LOFT
16⁰ x 6⁰

OPEN TO BELOW

40'-0''

UPPER LEVEL

A-frame Simplicity

No. 90025

It is no wonder that the unique look of an A-frame has proven to be a popular vacation design, since it is dramatic to look at, practical to live in and economical to build. Highlights of this design are the fieldstone chimney that soars up through the roof, vertical boards and battens, stained red-cedar wood shingles and a redwood sundeck that creates an interesting exterior. For year-round living, provision is made for a supplemental heating unit in the utility room. Although the plan is of basementless design, a full basement is possible if the physical land characteristics permit, with the basement stair located under the main stair where the closet is now shown.

First floor — 884 sq. ft.
Second floor — 441 sq. ft.
Deck — 364 sq. ft.

Total living area — 1,325 sq. ft.

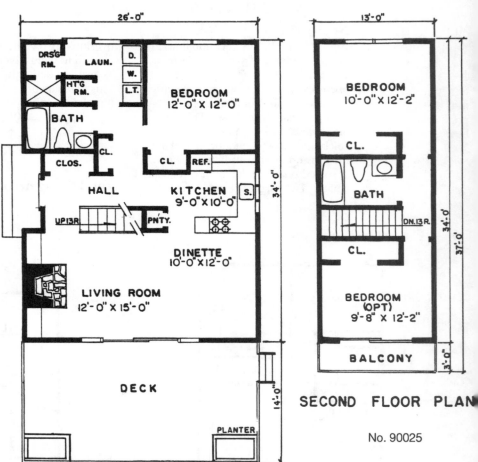

FIRST FLOOR PLAN

SECOND FLOOR PLAN

No. 90025

Three Porches Offer Outdoor Charm

No. 90048

Summer fun can be enhanced by the atmosphere this beautiful home provides. It has been designed so it can be used in winter and summer. A basement is provided that could be easily eliminated if not required. Three porches offer maximum outdoor living space. The one on the left is for clean up for the sportsman returning from his activities. A laundry with utility sink and a stall shower are provided, plus a closet for gear. The interior is as dramatic as the exterior. Note the oversized log burning fireplace on the right wall. Three bedrooms and two baths can be built by finishing the second floor. Note the U-shaped kitchen with adjoining dining porch.

First floor — 972 sq. ft.
Second floor w/ balcony — 321 sq. ft.
Total living area — 1,293 sq. ft.

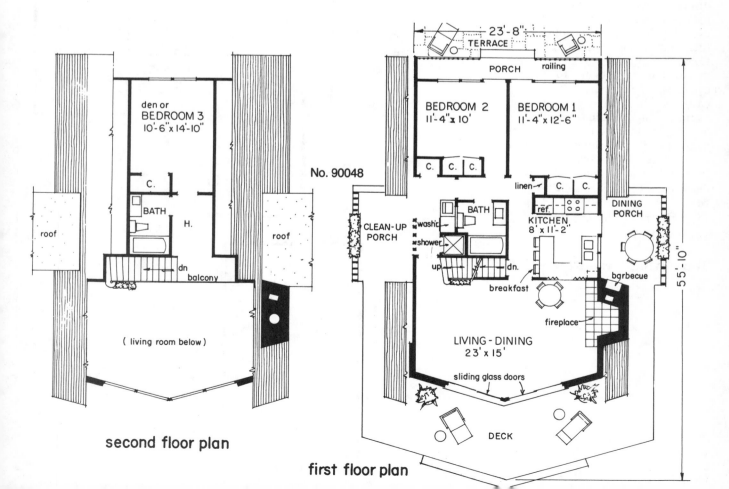

second floor plan

first floor plan

No. 90048

Contemporary Sophistication

No. 24307

When being quaint is not what you had in mind for your second home, may we make this suggestion. Take a look at the angles of the outside of this home....and that terrific roof line. No, this isn't grandma's cabin. You have today's style and sophistication in your everyday life, why not in your leisure life. In the living room the center fireplace is circular providing interest, to the room and ambiance to your evenings. The efficient kitchen flows easily into the dining area. For those warmer nights, the dining area accesses a deck. The main bedroom has its own bath complete with shower and ample closet space. The second bedroom is located close to the hall bath. Upstairs, the studio area overlooks the floor below.

First floor — 864 sq. ft.

Loft — 144 sq. ft.

Total living area — 864 sq. ft.

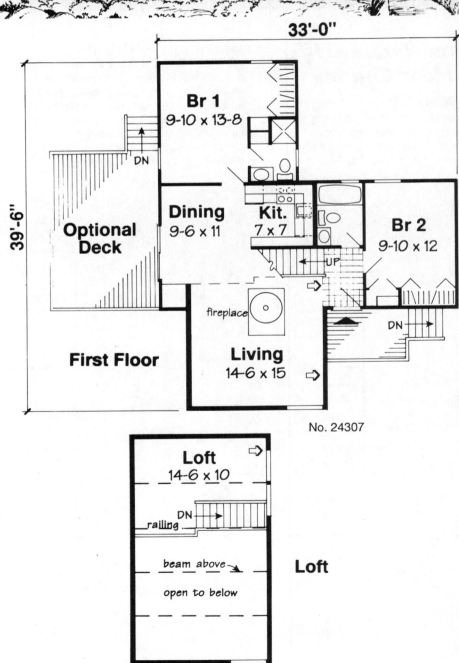

Modified A-Frame
At Home Anywhere

No. 90309

This compact plan for comfortable living is equally suitable in suburbia or a resort. The main floor includes a combined living room/dining room whose ceiling reaches to the second floor loft. This living area is further enhanced by its view of the angled deck through corner windows and two sliding glass doors, plus the fireplace with its large hearth. Located at one end of the rear deck is a roomy outdoor storage cabinet. The galley-style kitchen is conveniently arranged and is located near both the front entrance and the laundry area for convenience.

Completing the main floor are a bedroom and a full bath. In addition to the loft on the second floor, there is an optional bedroom and half-bath on this level.

Main Floor — 735 sq. ft.
Upper Floor — 304 sq. ft.

Total living area — 1,039 sq. ft.

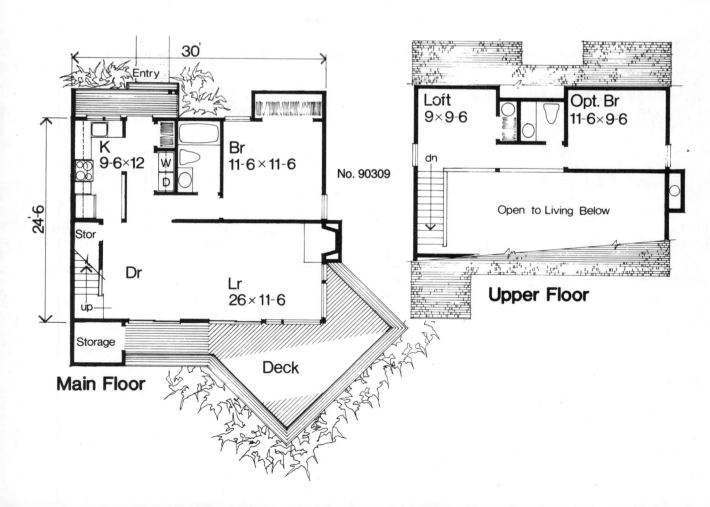

Main Floor

Upper Floor

Interesting Angles Add Style

No. 92804

This home has a style all its own with the use of angles and windows. The wood deck provides the entrance area. Once inside the home the living room is sunny and spacious with windows to the second floor. There is also a fireplace, providing warmth and atmosphere to the room. The kitchen/dining area also enjoys the use of angles in its shape. Efficiently layed out, the kitchen provides the cook of your family the room, cabinet space and appliances that allow less time preparing and more time relaxing and enjoying. There are two bedrooms on the first floor and a gorgeous master suite upstairs. The master suite includes a spa area and a private master bath. There is a balcony overlooking the living room. Style at every turn.

First floor — 1,051 sq. ft.
Second floor — 635 sq. ft.

Total living area — 1,686 sq. ft.

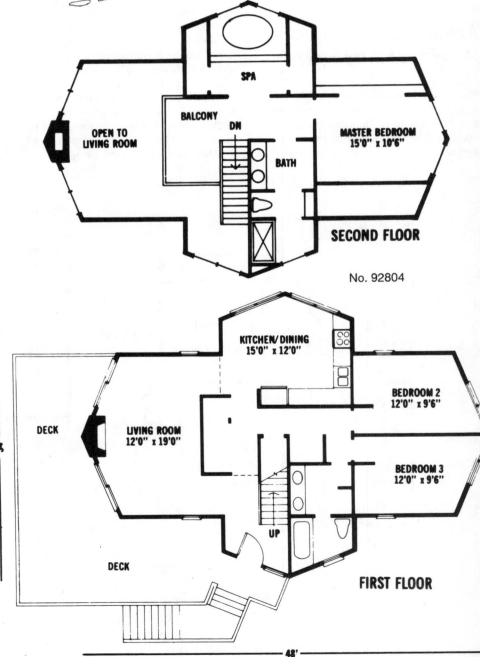

No. 92804

SPA
BALCONY
DN
OPEN TO LIVING ROOM
BATH
MASTER BEDROOM 15'0" x 10'6"
SECOND FLOOR

KITCHEN/DINING 15'0" x 12'0"
BEDROOM 2 12'0" x 9'6"
DECK
LIVING ROOM 12'0" x 19'0"
BEDROOM 3 12'0" x 9'6"
DECK
UP
FIRST FLOOR

34'

48'

Sunken Living Areas in Compact Plan

No. 26114

Step down from the entry-level to the sunken living, dining, and kitchen areas of this floor plan. The fireplaced living room looks out through double sliding glass doors to a wrap-around deck which ends in outside storage. Ceilings slope up above a balcony which also shares the second level with two bedrooms and a bath. An optional third bedroom/den lies on the lower level.

First floor — 696 sq. ft.
Second floor — 416 sq. ft.
Basement — 696 sq. ft.
Storage — 32 sq. ft.
Deck — 232 sq. ft.

Total living area — 1,112 sq. ft.

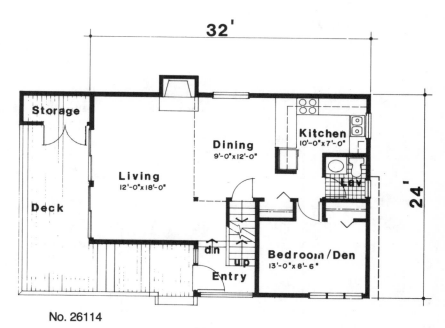

No. 26114

FIRST FLOOR

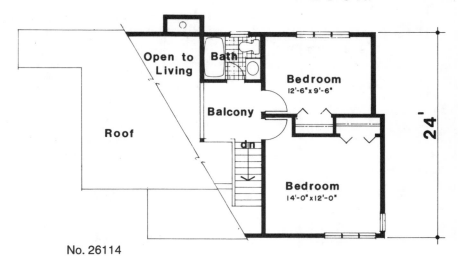

No. 26114

SECOND FLOOR

Rustic Design Blends with Hillside

No. 10012

Naturally perfect for a woodland setting, this redwood decked home will adapt equally well to a lake or ocean setting. A car or boat garage is furnished on the lower level. Fireplaces equip both the living room and the 36-foot long family room which opens onto a shaded patio. A laundry room adjoins the open kitchen which shares the large redwood deck encircling the living and dining area. Two bedrooms and two full baths on the first floor supplement another bedroom and half bath on the lower level.

Main living area — 1,198 sq. ft.
Basement — 1,198 sq. ft.

Total living area — 1,198 sq. ft.

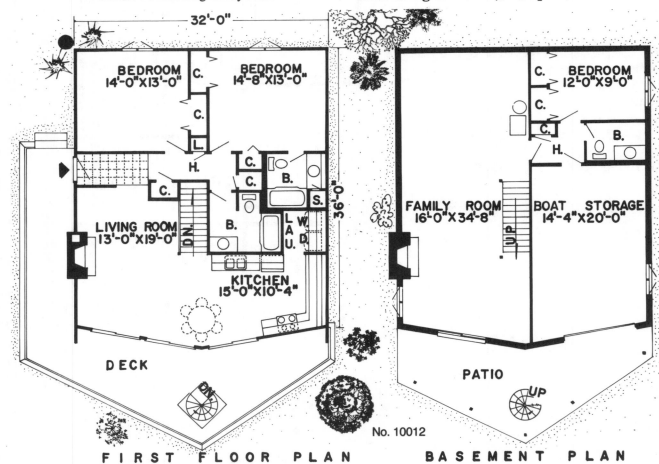

No. 10012

FIRST FLOOR PLAN   BASEMENT PLAN

Versatile Chalet

No. 90171

Capture the spirit of the woods with this vacation classic. Designed as a hideaway for two (note the single bathroom), this plan adds extra bedrooms upstairs for occasional family or guests. The large living room joins the deck through sliding doors. An efficient eat-in kitchen keeps cleanup to a minimum. The stone fireplace and rustic, shingled exterior add plenty of deep-in-the-woods charm. This plan is available with a basement or crawl space/pier and beam foundation. Please specify when ordering.

First Floor — 780 sq. ft.
Second Floor — 500 sq. ft.
Basement — 780 sq. ft.

Total living area — 1,280 sq. ft.

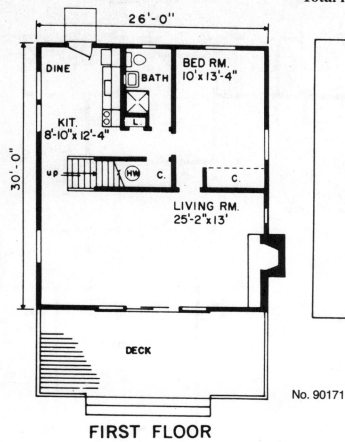

26'-0"

30'-0"

DINE

KIT.
8'-10"x12'-4"

BATH

BED RM.
10'x13'-4"

up

HW

C.

C.

LIVING RM.
25'-2"x13'

DECK

FIRST FLOOR

No. 90171

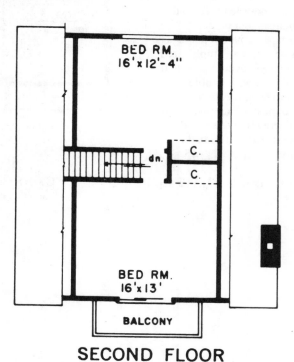

BED RM.
16'x12'-4"

dn.

C.

C.

BED RM.
16'x13'

BALCONY

SECOND FLOOR

Easy Living Design

No. 91342

All amenities of modern home planning have been incorporated into this plan. Perfect for vacation, year-round, or retirement, this house was designed with the handicapped in mind. The vaulted Great room, dining and kitchen areas create a feeling of spaciousness, while lending to a relaxed atmosphere. The kitchen, accented with angles, has an abundance of cabinets for storage and is enhanced by a tiled work island. A sliding glass door leads from the Great room areas to a unique triangular-shaped covered deck. The master bedroom has an ample sized wardrobe, a large covered private deck, and personal bath with double-sink vanity and tub bench. A non-handicapped master bath plan is also available. There are two secondary bedrooms that share a full bath.

Main living area — 1,345 sq. ft.

Total living area — 1,345 sq. ft.

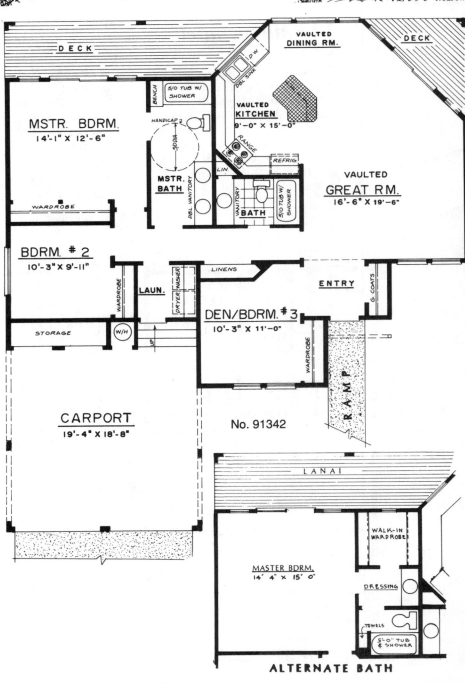

Cozy and Comfortable

No. 90523

Whenever it rains or snows, you'll appreciate the thoughtfulness of this design as you go directly from your two car garage into the interior. Curled up in the den, or in front of the fireplace, you'll be content. When guests come, they'll enjoy the privacy of their bedroom and bathroom. When you see your handsome double master bedroom windows with overhead fanlight from outside, or look through from inside, you'll appreciate the thoughtful design. And when you look into your pocketbook after you have built, you may feel downright brilliant.

Main living area — 1,350 sq. ft.
Garage — 2 car

Total living area — 1,350 sq. ft.

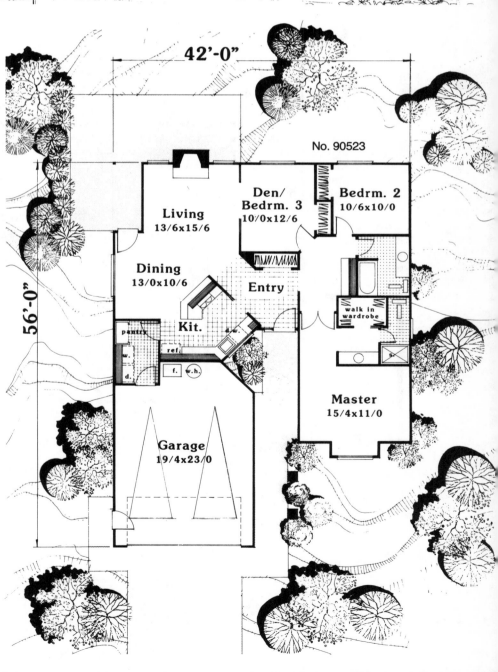

No. 90523

42'-0"

56'-0"

Living
13/6x15/6

Dining
13/0x10/6

Kit.

pantry

w.

d.

ref.

f. w.h.

Den/
Bedrm. 3
10/0x12/6

Entry

Bedrm. 2
10/6x10/0

walk in
wardrobe

Master
15/4x11/0

Garage
19/4x23/0

Leave Your Cares Behind

No. 91031

All you'll have to do in this snug retreat is relax and enjoy the view. Outside on your deck or inside looking though the three large windows or the double glass living room door, you'll appreciate the wonders of nature. But you won't be roughing it. You'll enjoy the cozy bedroom, comforts like a hot shower, and the joys of cooking in a kitchen open to the two-story living space. If you do invite guests to this cottage to share your privacy, they can bed down upstairs in the loft bedroom. This plan is available with a crawl space foundation only.

Main Level — 572 sq. ft.
Loft — 308 sq. ft.
Total living area — 880 sq. ft.

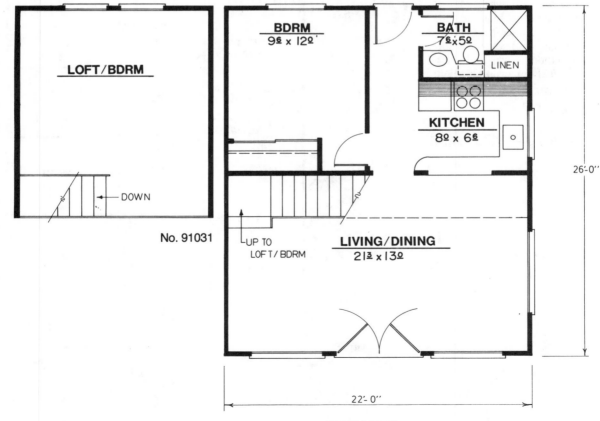

LOFT/BDRM

DOWN

No. 91031

BDRM
9⁶ x 12⁰

BATH
7⁶ x 5⁰

LINEN

KITCHEN
8⁰ x 6⁶

UP TO
LOFT/BDRM

LIVING/DINING
21³ x 13⁰

26'-0"

22'-0"

MAIN LEVEL

Suited for a Hill

No. 90822

Use this compact A-frame year round or as a vacation retreat. Either way, this practical design is bound to give you pleasure for a long, long time. The main floor, with its vaulted ceilings and fieldstone fireplace, combines kitchen, living and dining rooms with two bedrooms and a full bath. The wrap-around sundeck affords lots of outdoor living space. With its soaring views of the floor below, the loft contains the master suite and the perfect place for a home office.

Main floor area — 925 sq. ft.
Loft — 338 sq. ft.
Basement — 864 sq. ft.
Width — 33'-0"
Depth — 47'-0"

Total living area — 1,263 sq. ft.

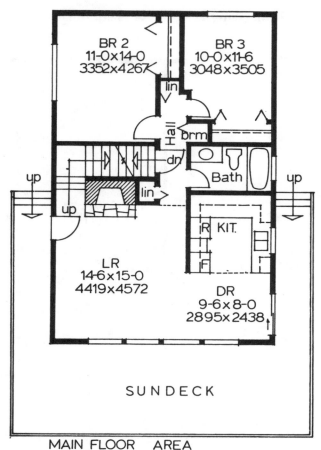

MAIN FLOOR   AREA

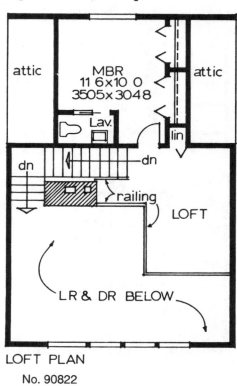

LOFT PLAN
No. 90822

Tailored to Fit

No. 90168

Here's a skier's delight: a classic cabin whose looks echo the beauty of the mountains. This well designed plan will comfortably fit a houseful of guests. The first-floor plan places a huge room in front of the roaring fireplace, warming and soothing to all. The step-saving kitchen can toss out a lot of food in a short time, and snackers and helpers can sit at the bar. The downstairs bedroom is supplemented by a bunk room. Upstairs, two large bedrooms have plenty of closet space. The charming exterior features the deck and the shingle finish...not to mention a touch of the Alps. This plan is available with a crawl space foundation only.

First floor — 884 sq. ft.
Second floor — 550 sq. ft.

Total living area — 1,434 sq. ft.

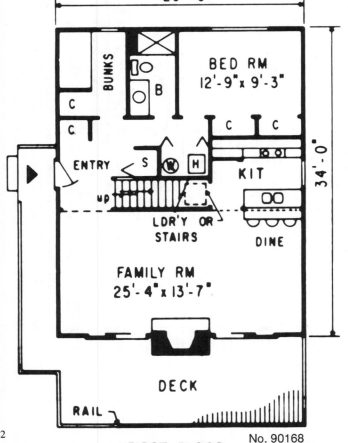

FIRST FLOOR   No. 90168

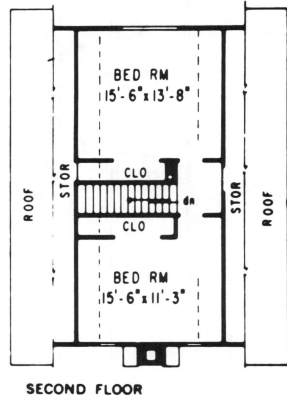

SECOND FLOOR

Dinner on the Deck

No. 90669

Enjoy rugged good looks, and practical features, whether you build this as a first or second home. Cut down your heating bills in this rugged, contemporary energy-saver with an efficient wood stove. An ingenious design allows warm air to rise through wooden louvers from the two-story living room to the bedrooms upstairs . If this is your beachfront or mountaintop dream house, you'll appreciate the built-in window seats, handy for extra guests. And, four outdoor decks insure you'll never run out of room. Don't worry about tracking through the house; there's a shower just off the mudroom. A full bath and deck adjoin the first floor bedroom. Upstairs, two more bedrooms and another full bath complete this compact gem.

First floor — 877 sq. ft.
Second floor — 455 sq. ft.

Total living area — 1,332 sq. ft.

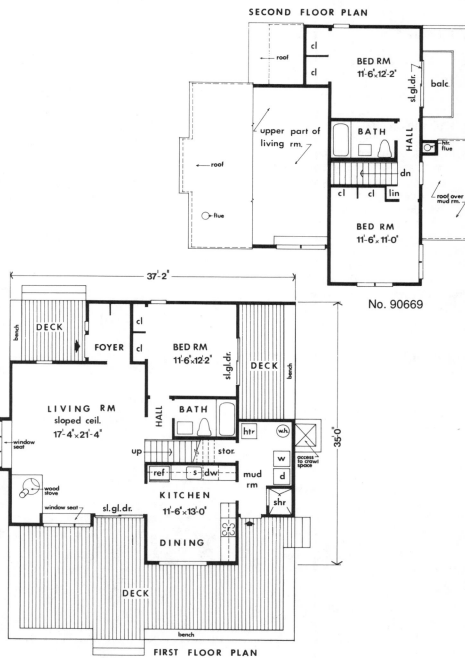

SECOND FLOOR PLAN

No. 90669

FIRST FLOOR PLAN

Compact Plan Yields Lots of Living Space

No. 10519

The sloped ceilings of this well-designed home's living and dining rooms, plus the central, open stairway, create a spacious, inviting living area. The efficient, U-shaped kitchen is well located with access to the dining room, the laundry area and the lavatory. It has direct access outside, too, so bringing in the groceries is less of a chore. The first floor bedroom has double closets and a private bath. The two second floor bedrooms share a bath on the upstairs hall where two large linen closets are located. Each bedroom has ample closet space.

First floor — 872 sq. ft.
Second floor — 483 sq. ft.

Total living area — 1,355 sq. ft.

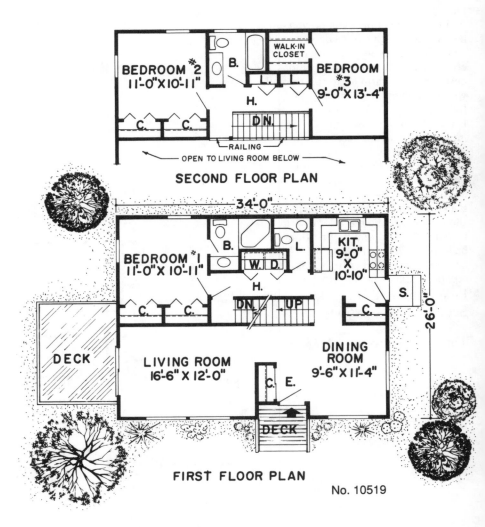

No. 10519

Cabin in the Country

No. 90433

Enjoy an up-to-date improvement on a vacation classic. You'll like the echoes of the past in this rustic looking, easy-to-maintain cabin, while you'll love the modern touches like 1-1/2 baths. The large screened porch invites you to relax or eat in style and take advantage of this country comfort. If the air gets nippy, you may want to sit by the fire in the cozy living room. Or, snuggle up in one of two bedrooms, each with its own bathroom. If you've overdone your outside exploring, a long, hot bath will restore you. This design, similar to classic cabins of the past, will always be a joy. This plan is available with a slab or crawl space foundation. Please specify when ordering.

Main living area — 928 sq. ft.
Screen porch — 230 sq. ft.
Storage area — 14 sq. ft.

Total living area — 928 sq. ft.

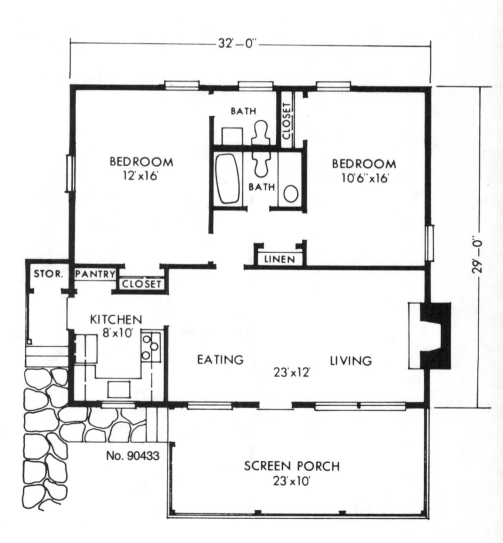

A Nest for Empty-Nesters

No. 90934

Modest in size, this one floor house has many amenities. With no basement, it will be very economical to build. A mudroom/laundry inside the side door traps dirt before it can enter the house. The living room, dining area, and kitchen all look out on the covered deck which adds real space to this carefree, budget conscience home.

Main living area — 884 sq. ft.
Width — 34'-0"
Depth — 28'-0"

Total living area — 884 sq. ft.

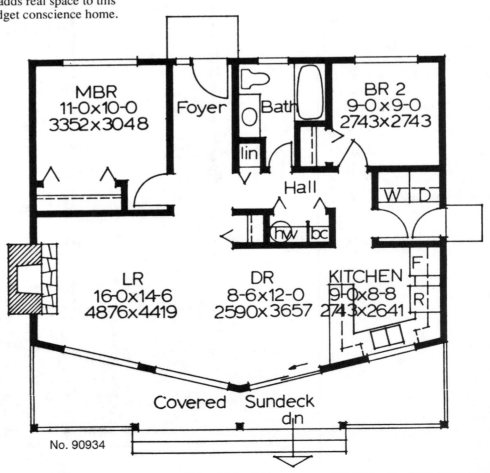

GARAGE PLANS

Save money by Doing-It-Yourself using our Easy-To-Follow plans. Whether you intend to build your own garage or contract it out to a building professional, the Garlinghouse garage plans provide you with everything you need to price out your project and get started. Put our 85 years of experience to work for you.
Order now!!

ITEM NO. 06016C — $86.00
Apartment Garage With One Bedroom

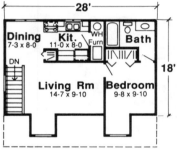

- 24' x 28' Overall Dimensions
- 544 Square Foot Apartment
- 12/12 Gable Roof with Dormers
- Slab or Stem Wall Foundation Options

ITEM NO. 06015C — $86.00
Apartment Garage With Two Bedrooms

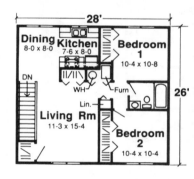

- 26' x 28' Overall Dimensions
- 728 Square Foot Apartment
- 4/12 Pitch Gable Roof
- Slab or Stem Wall Foundation Options

ITEM NO. 06012C — $54.00
30' Deep Gable &/or Eave Jumbo Garages

- 4/12 Pitch Gable Roof
- Available Options for Extra Tall Walls, Garage & Personnel Doors, Foundation, Window, & Sidings
- Package contains 4 Different Sizes
  - 30' x 28' • 30' x 32' • 30' x 36' • 30' x 40'

ITEM NO. 06013C — $68.00
Two-Car Garage With Mudroom/Breezeway

- Attaches to Any House
- 24' x 24' Eave Entry
- Available Options for Utility Room with Bath, Mudroom, Screened-In Breezeway, Roof, Foundation, Garage & Personnel Doors, Window, & Sidings

ITEM NO. 06001C — $48.00
12', 14', & 16' Wide-Gable 1-Car Garages

- Available Options for Roof, Foundation, Window, Door, & Sidings
- Package contains 8 Different Sizes
- 12' x 20' Mini-Garage • 14' x 22' • 16' x 20' • 16' x 24'
- 14' x 20' • 14' x 24' • 16' x 22' • 16' x 26'

ITEM NO. 06003C — $48.00
24' Wide-Gable 2-Car Garages

- Available Options for Side Shed, Roof, Foundation, Garage & Personnel Doors, Window, & Sidings
- Package contains 5 Different Sizes
- 24' x 22' • 24' x 24' • 24' x 26'
- 24' x 28' • 24' x 32'

ITEM NO. 06007C — $60.00
Gable 2-Car Gambrel Roof Garages

- Interior Rear Stairs to Loft Workshop
- Front Loft Cargo Door With Pulley Lift
- Available Options for Foundation, Garage & Personnel Doors, Window, & Sidings
- Package contains 5 Different Sizes
- 22' x 26' • 22' x 28' • 24' x 28' • 24' x 30' • 24' x 32'

ITEM NO. 06006C — $48.00
22' & 24' Deep Eave 2 & 3-Car Garages

- Can Be Built Stand-Alone or Attached to House
- Available Options for Roof, Foundation, Garage & Personnel Doors, Window, & Sidings
- Package contains 6 Different Sizes
- 22' x 28' • 22' x 32' • 24' x 32'
- 22' x 30' • 24' x 30' • 24' x 36'

ITEM NO. 06002C — $48.00
20' & 22' Wide-Gable 2-Car Garages

- Available Options for Roof, Foundation, Garage & Personnel Doors, Window, & Sidings
- Package contains 7 Different Sizes
- 20' x 20' • 20' x 24' • 22' x 22' • 22' x 28'
- 20' x 22' • 20' x 28' • 22' x 24'

ITEM NO. 06008C — $60.00
Eave 2 & 3-Car Clerestory Roof Garages

- Interior Side Stairs to Loft Workshop
- Available Options for Engine Lift, Foundation, Garage & Personnel Doors, Window, & Sidings
- Package contains 4 Different Sizes
- 24' x 26' • 24' x 28' • 24' x 32' • 24' x 36'

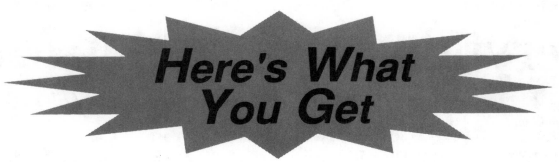

Here's What You Get

- Three complete sets of drawings for each plan ordered.
- Detailed step-by-step instructions with easy-to-follow diagrams on how to build your garage (not available with apartment/garages).
- For each garage style, a variety of size and garage door configuration options.
- Variety of roof styles and/or pitch options for most garages.

- Complete materials list.
- Choice between three foundation options: Monolithic Slab, Concrete Stem Wall or Concrete Block Stem Wall.
- Full framing plans, elevations and cross-sectionals for each garage size and configuration.
- And Much More!!

Order Information For Garage Plans:

All garage plan orders contain three complete sets of drawings with instructions and are priced as listed next to the illustration. Additional sets of plans may be obtained for $10.00 each with your original order. UPS shipping is used unless otherwise requested. Please include the proper amount for shipping.

GARLINGHOUSE
Build-It-Yourself
PROJECT PLAN

Garage Order Form

Order Code No. G3VL3

Please send me 3 complete sets of the following *GARAGE PLAN*:

Item no. & description	Price
_____	$_____
Additional Sets	
_____ (@ $10.00 each)	$_____
Shipping Charges: UPS-$3.75, First Class- $4.50	$_____
Subtotal:	$_____
Resident sales tax: KS-5.9%, CT-6%	$_____
Total Enclosed:	$_____

Send your order to:
(With check or money order payable in U.S. funds only)
The Garlinghouse Company
34 Industrial Park Place
P.O. Box 1717
Middletown, CT 06457

No C.O.D. orders accepted; U.S. funds only. UPS will not ship to Post Office boxes, FPO boxes, APO boxes, Alaska or Hawaii. Canadian orders must be shipped First Class.

Prices subject to change without notice.

My Billing Address is:
Name _____
Address _____
City _____
State _____ Zip _____
Daytime Phone No. _____

My Shipping Address is:
Name _____
Address _____
(UPS will not ship to P.O. Boxes)
City _____
State _____ Zip _____

For Faster Service...Charge It!
U.S. & Canada Call
1(800)235-5700
All foreign residents call 1(203)632-0500
❑ Mastercard ❑ Visa ❑ Discover

Card # | | | | | | | | | | | | | | | | |

Signature _____ Exp.___/___

If paying by credit card, to avoid delays:
billing address must be as it appears on credit card statement
or FAX us at (203) 632-0712

Everything You Need to Make

You pay only a fraction of the original cost

You've picked your dream home!

You can already see it standing on your lot... you can see your-selves in your new home... enjoying family, entertaining guests, cele-brating holidays. All that remains ahead are the details. That's where we can help. Whether you plan to build-it-yourself, be your own contractor, or hand your plans over to an outside contractor, your Garlinghouse blueprints provide the perfect beginning for putting yourself in your dream home right away.

We even make it simple for you to make professional design modi-fications. We can also provide a materials list for greater economy.

My grandfather, L.F. Garlinghouse, started a tradition of quality when he founded this company in 1907. For over 85 years, homeown-ers and builders have relied on us for accurate, complete, professional blueprints. Our plans help you get results fast... and save money, too! These pages will give you all the information you need to order. So get started now... I know you'll love your new Garlinghouse home!

Sincerely,

HERE'S WHAT YOU GET!

Exterior Elevations

Exact scale views of the front, rear and both sides of your home, showing exterior materials, details, and all necessary measurements.

Detailed Floor Plans

Showing the placement of all interior walls, the dimensions of rooms, doors, win-dows, stairways, and other details.

Typical Wall Sections

Detailed views of your exterior walls, as though sliced from top to bottom. These drawings clarify exterior wall construction insulation, flooring, and roofing details. Depending on your specific geography and climate, your home will be built with either 2x4 or 2x6 exterior walls. Most profes-sional contractors can easily adapt plans for either requirement.

Kitchen and Bath Cabinet Details

These plans or, in some cases, elevations show the specific details and placement of the cabinets in your kitchen and bathrooms as applicable. Customizing these areas is simpler beginning with these details

140

Your Dream Come True!

for home designs by respected professionals.

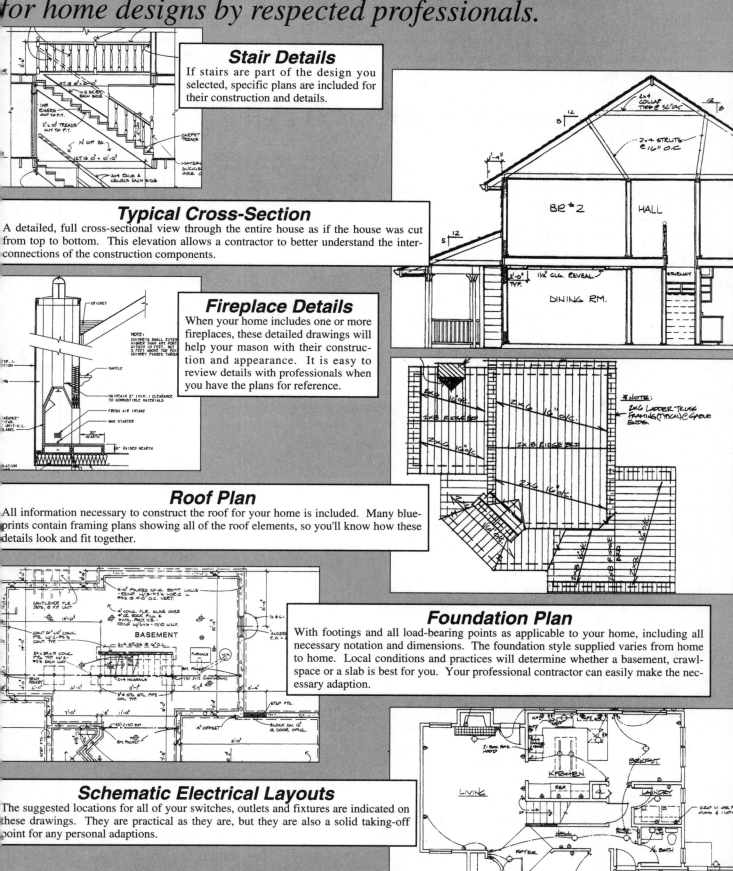

Stair Details

If stairs are part of the design you selected, specific plans are included for their construction and details.

Typical Cross-Section

A detailed, full cross-sectional view through the entire house as if the house was cut from top to bottom. This elevation allows a contractor to better understand the inter-connections of the construction components.

Fireplace Details

When your home includes one or more fireplaces, these detailed drawings will help your mason with their construction and appearance. It is easy to review details with professionals when you have the plans for reference.

Roof Plan

All information necessary to construct the roof for your home is included. Many blue-prints contain framing plans showing all of the roof elements, so you'll know how these details look and fit together.

Foundation Plan

With footings and all load-bearing points as applicable to your home, including all necessary notation and dimensions. The foundation style supplied varies from home to home. Local conditions and practices will determine whether a basement, crawl-space or a slab is best for you. Your professional contractor can easily make the necessary adaption.

Schematic Electrical Layouts

The suggested locations for all of your switches, outlets and fixtures are indicated on these drawings. They are practical as they are, but they are also a solid taking-off point for any personal adaptions.

Garlinghouse options and extras make the dream truly yours.

Reversed Plans Can Make Your Dream Home Just Right!

"That's our dream home... if only the garage were on the other side!"

You could have exactly the home you want by flipping it end-for-end. Check it out by holding your dream home page of this book up to a mirror. Then simply order your plans "reversed". We'll send you one full set of mirror-image plans (with the writing backwards) as a master guide for you and your builder.

The remaining sets of your order will come as shown in this book so the dimensions and specifications are easily read on the job site... but they will be specially stamped "REVERSED" so there is no construction confusion.

We can only send reversed plans with multiple-set orders. But, there is no extra charge for this service.

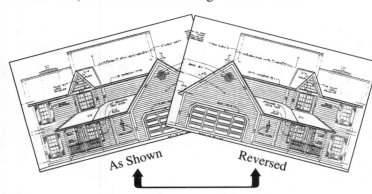

As Shown   Reversed

Modifying Your Garlinghouse Home Plan

Easy modifications to your dream home... minor non-structural changes, simple material substitutions... can be made between you and your builder.

However, if you are considering making major changes to your design, we strongly recommend that you use an architect or a professional designer. And, since you have already started with our complete detailed blueprints, the cost of those expensive professional services will be significantly less.

Our Reproducible Vellums Make Modifications Easier

They provide a design professional with the right way to make changes directly to your Garlinghouse home plans and then print as many copies of the modified plans as you need. The price is $395 plus shipping. Call 1-800-235-5700 to find out more.

Yours FREE With Your Order

FREE
SPECIFICATIONS AND CONTRACT FORM provides the perfect way for you and your builder to agree on the exact materials to use in building and finishing your home *before* you start construction. A must for homeowner's peace of mind.

FREE
14-PAGE ENERGY CONSERVATION SPEC-IFICATIONS GUIDE puts you "in the know" for specifying the energy conserving materials and methods appropriate for your climate. It includes an easy to use R-values chart to maximize energy savings.

Remember To Order Your Materials List

It'll help you save money. Available at a modest additional charge, the Materials List gives the quantity, dimensions, and specifications for the major materials needed to build your home. You will get faster, more accurate bids from your contractors and building suppliers — and avoid paying for unused materials and waste. Materials Lists are available for all home plans except as otherwise indicated but can only be ordered with a set of home plans. Due to differences in regional requirements and homeowner or builder preferences... electrical, plumbing and heating/air conditioning equipment specifications are not designed specifically for each plan. However, detailed *typical* prints of residential electrical, plumbing and construction guidelines can be provided. Each set of electrical and plumbing prints conforms to the requirements at the National Electrical and Plumbing Codes. The construction prints conform to the Uniform Building Code or BOCA code. These prints can be supplied at a low cost of $14.95 each.

Questions?
Call our customer service number at 1-203-632-0500.

How Many Sets Of Plans Will You Need?

The Standard 8-Set Construction Package

Our experience shows that you'll speed every step of construction and avoid costly building errors by ordering enough sets to go around. Each tradesperson wants a set — the general contractor and all subcontractors; foundation, electrical, plumbing, heating/air conditioning, drywall, finish carpenters, and cabinet shop. Don't forget your lending institution, building department and, of course, a set for yourself.

The Minimum 5-Set Construction Package

If you're comfortable with arduous follow-up, this package can save you a few dollars by giving you the option of passing down plan sets as work progresses. You might have enough copies to go around if work goes exactly as scheduled and no plans are lost or damaged. But for only $30 more, the 8-set package eliminates these worries.

The Single-Set Decision-Maker Package

We offer this set so you can study the blueprints to plan your dream home in detail. But remember... one set is never enough to build your home... and they're copyrighted.

New Plan Details For The Home Builder

Because local codes and requirements vary greatly, we recommend that you obtain drawings and bids from licensed contractors to do your mechanical plans. However, if you want to know more about techniques — and deal more confidently with subcontractors — we offer these remarkably useful detail sheets. Each is an excellent tool that will enhance your understanding of these technical subjects.

Residential Construction Details

Eight sheets that cover the essentials of stick-built residential home construction. Details foundation options - poured concrete basement, concrete block, or monolithic

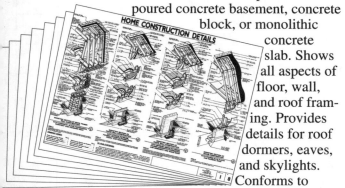

concrete slab. Shows all aspects of floor, wall, and roof framing. Provides details for roof dormers, eaves, and skylights. Conforms to requirements of Uniform Building code or BOCA code. Includes a quick index. *$14.95 per set*

Residential Plumbing Details

Nine sheets packed with information detailing pipe connection methods, fittings, and sizes. Shows sump-pump and water softener hookups, and septic system construction. Conforms to requirements

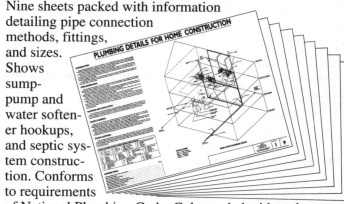

of National Plumbing Code. Color coded with a glossary of terms and quick index. *$14.95 per set*

Residential Electrical Details

Nine sheets that cover all aspects of residential wiring, from simple switch wiring to the complexities of three-phase and service entrance connection. Explains service load calculations and distribution panel wiring. Shows you how to create a floor-plan wiring diagram. Conforms to requirements of

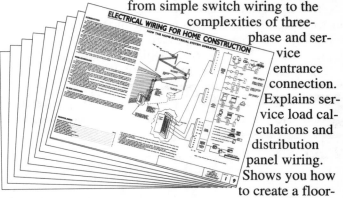

National Electrical Code. Color coded with a glossary of terms and a quick index. *$14.95 per set*

Important Shipping Information

Your order is processed immediately. Allow 10 working days from our receipt of your order for normal UPS delivery. Save time with your credit card and our "800" number. UPS *must* have a street address or Rural Route Box number — never a post office box. Use a work address if no one is home during the day.

Orders being shipped to Alaska, Hawaii, APO, FPO or Post Office Boxes must go via First Class Mail. Please include the proper postage.

Overseas checks, money orders, or international money transfers must be payable in U.S. currency. For speed, we ship international orders Air Parcel Post. Please refer to the chart for the correct shipping cost.

An important note:

All plans are drawn to conform to one or more of the industry's major national building standards. However, due to the variety of local building regulations, your plan may need to be modified to comply with local requirements — snow loads, energy loads, seismic zones, etc. Do check them fully and consult your local building officials.

A few states require that all building plans used be drawn by an architect registered in that state. While having your plans reviewed and stamped by such an architect may be prudent, laws requiring non-conforming plans like ours to be completely redrawn forces you to unnecessarily pay very large fees. If your state has such a law, we strongly recommend you contact your state representative to protest.

Blueprint Price Schedule

Standard Construction Package (8 sets)	$255.00
Minimum Construction Package (5 sets)	$225.00
Single-Set Package	$180.00
Each Additional Set (ordered w/one above)	$ 20.00
Materials List (with plan order only)	$ 25.00

Domestic Shipping

UPS Ground Service	$ 7.00
First Class Mail	$ 8.50

Express Delivery Service — Call For Details 1-800-235-5700

International Shipping	One Set	Mult. Sets
Canada	$ 7.25	$12.50
Carribean Nations & Mexico	$16.50	$39.50
All Other Nations	$18.50	$50.00

Canadian orders are now Duty Free.

Canadian Orders and Shipping:

To our friends in Canada, we have a plan design affiliate in Kitchener, Ontario. This relationship will help you avoid the delays and charges associated with shipments from the United States. Moreover, our affiliate is familiar with the building requirements in your community and country.

We prefer payments in U.S. Currency. If you, however, are sending Canadian funds please add 30% to the prices of the plans and shipping fees.

Please Submit all Canadian plan orders to:

The Garlinghouse Company, Inc.
20 Cedar Street North
Kitchener, Ontario N2H, 2W8

Canadian orders only: 1-800-561-4169
Fax #: 1-519-743-1282
Customer Service #: 1-519-743-4169

Before ordering **PLEASE READ** *all ordering information*

ORDER TOLL FREE
1-800-235-5700
Monday-Friday 8:00 a.m. to 5:00 p.m. Eastern Time
or FAX your Credit Card order to 1-203-632-0712
Connecticut, Alaska, Hawaii, and all foreign residents
call 1-203-632-0500.

Please have ready:

1. Your credit card number
2. The plan number
3. The order code number

Blueprint Order Form

GARLINGHOUSE

Prices Guaranteed until: 1-6-94

Order Code No. **H3VL3**

Plan No. _____
❏ As Shown ❏ Reversed *(mult. set pkgs. only)*

	Each	Amount
8 set pkg.	$255.00	$
5 set pkg.	$225.00	$
1 set pkg. (no reverses)	$180.00	$
_____ (qty.) Add'l. sets @	$ 20.00	$
Material List	$ 25.00	$
Residential Builder Plans		
_____ set(s) Construction @	$ 14.95	$
_____ set(s) Plumbing @	$ 14.95	$
_____ set(s) Electrical @	$ 14.95	$
Shipping — see chart		$
Subtotal		$
Sales Tax (CT residents add 6% sales tax, KS residents add 5.9% sales tax)		$
Total Amount Enclosed		*$*

Thank your for your order!

Garlinghouse plans are copyright protected. Purchaser hereby agrees that the home plan construction drawings being purchased will not be used for the construction of more than one single dwelling, and that these drawings will not be reproduced either in whole or in part by any means whatsoever.

Send your check, money order or credit card information to:
Garlinghouse Company
34 Industrial Park Place, P.O. Box 1717
Middletown, CT 06457

Bill To: (address must be as it appears on credit card statement)

Name _____
Please Print

Address _____

City/State _____ Zip _____

Daytime Phone ( ) _____

Ship To (if different from Bill to):

Name _____

Address _____
UPS will not ship to P.O. Boxes

City/State _____ Zip _____

Credit Card Information

Charge To: ❏ Visa ❏ Mastercard ❏ Discover

Card # ⌊⌋⌊⌋⌊⌋⌊⌋⌊⌋⌊⌋⌊⌋⌊⌋⌊⌋⌊⌋⌊⌋⌊⌋⌊⌋⌊⌋⌊⌋⌊⌋

Signature _____ Exp. ___/___